THE REAL

PARISH

TED & JOAN FLAXMAN

FOREWORD BY SIR HUGO BRUNNER

First published in Great Britain 2009
By E W Flaxman, The Old School, Cottisford, Oxfordshire, NN13 5SW

ISBN 978-0-9548986-3-2

Printed and bound by Information Press Ltd, Eynsham, Oxford

Design by Cox Design Ltd, Witney, Oxon

FOREWORD

What a pleasure it is to commend this book about the Oxfordshire parish in which Flora Thompson was born. Were it not for her, we would perhaps have been deprived of these fascinating stories. But, of course, Ted and Joan Flaxman have done all the careful research and presented it to us in a delightful way. I have relished in particular the occasional comments on these tales of Cottisford families – they are imbued with Flora's shrewdness and commonsense.

Their work is obviously a labour of love, following as it does their publication of "Cottisford Revisited" and their initiation of the first performance of the play "Lark Rise" in the hamlet of Juniper Hill. I was moved by that performance as by no other. And something that Keith Dewhurst said after it moved me too: "Flora Thompson reminds us that we are more valuable than the machines we tend and that every forgotten person who lived is worthy of our remembrance and our honour". I have felt that intensely in reading again, as this book has prompted me to do, about Flora Thompson and her neighbours. They were so admirable in making the most of a few worldly goods, and in their "unflinching" approach to life, something we need to be reminded of today.

I became involved with Flora, and met her great champion, Margaret Lane, through being head of the department at OUP which published her books at the time when there was a revival of interest in her writing in the late 1970s. Now my interest is being renewed. In May this year, our son Magnus married a Texan. The wedding was in Oxford but, later this year, we will visit his bride's home town, Dallas. While we are there we will be lucky enough to be taken to see the Flora Thompson papers in the Harry Ransom Humanities Research Centre at the University of Texas at Austin.

"The Real Lark Rise Parish" will surely draw people to read or to reread Flora Thompson's books. But, if she were reading this, she would be very pleased that Ted and Joan have been able to tell us so much about Cottisford people, of whom she herself knew little or who, like Air Chief Marshal Sir Robert Brooke-Popham and Guardsman Ron Watts, lived in the parish after her time.

Hugo Brunner
August 2009

CONTENTS

1. INTRODUCTION

We have inserted the word "Real" into the title of this book because some viewers of the two recent BBC TV series entitled "Lark Rise to Candleford" do not realise, until they come here, that the actual Parish in Oxfordshire where Flora Thompson was born and brought up is very different from the "set" in Wiltshire on which the BBC's episodes have been filmed.

Those who have read the books are generally reassured to find the places of which she wrote so little changed. When she was describing Juniper Hill (her Lark Rise) in the second book of her trilogy in 1941 she wrote[1] that "No cottage had been added to the little group in the fields for many years, and, as it turned out, none were to be added for at least a half century; perhaps never, for the hamlet stands today unchanged in its outward appearance". Another 60 years have passed since she wrote that, and the hamlet is still largely as she described it – "unchanged in its outward appearance".

This is partly due to Flora herself. Local planning policies and decisions have been much influenced by her unique account of life here in the 19th Century. Although many of the houses at Juniper Hill have been extended and modernised internally, and all the thatches except one have gone, they are still, as she wrote[2], "not built in rows, but dotted down anywhere within a more or less circular group". The allotments, which were such an important source of produce for families during the hungry years, are still there and round the main group of houses is the unsurfaced private road along which people can still walk[3] "round the Rise". In the "mother village" of Cottisford (Flora's Fordlow) the school, the farm, the squire's house and, of course, the church can still be readily identified.

In the Introduction to her book[4] "A thousand years of the English Parish" Anthea Jones reminds the reader that "For many centuries, the parish provided an unchanging framework to everyday life: people belonged to a parish". And many aspects of their lives were largely governed by Parish Officials – the Clerk, the Constables, the Churchwardens, the Surveyor, the Overseers of the Poor – together, of course, with the Vicar and the Squire, Although the powers and duties of Parish authorities have declined greatly in the last 150 years the ancient Parish boundaries are largely unchanged and the identity and centrality of the Parish remains strong, particularly in many rural areas. People still feel that they belong to the Parish in which they live.

Our first booklet[5] on the history of the Parish, "Cottisford Revisited", is now in its second edition, the first edition having sold out in 2007. We hope this further booklet will prove of interest, not only in relation to Flora Thompson, but also in illustrating the extraordinary durability of this one typical, but unique, rural Parish.

2. TEN CENTURIES OF HISTORY

Cottisford is a small, relatively undistinguished, Parish in north Oxfordshire but it has been fortunate in its historians. Pride of place obviously goes to Flora Thompson, born Flora Jane Timms in the hamlet of Juniper Hill in 1877, whose autobiographical novel[6n] "Lark Rise" – the first book of her trilogy – provides a fascinating glimpse of what life was like for "ordinary folk" here during her childhood.

She wrote of a period when the old, settled, way of life in the countryside was beginning to change. When the centuries-old dominance of agriculture in everyday life was just starting to wane, and she recorded the experiences of poor families in a style which is both human in scale and convincing to read.

This is no dry-as-dust tome, but a small gem of social history. Its use as a "set book" for GCSE examinations in several years introduced "Lark Rise" to generations of youngsters who might never have come across it otherwise. And the BBC's two TV series in 2008 and 2009 have encouraged many new readers. With well over a million copies of the book sold, and translation into several foreign languages, "Lark Rise" has drawn the Parish to the attention of a great many people. Visitors come to savour the unchanged physical setting of "The Rise" at Juniper Hill: or to sit quietly in the tiny church where the brass War Memorial above her family pew provides a stark reminder of the poignant final paragraph[7] of the book in which Flora records the death on the battlefield of Flanders of her much-loved brother, Edwin Timms.

The other notable historian of the Parish is not so widely known. Rev J C Blomfield was one of that distinctive class of rural parsons in the 18th and 19th Centuries who combined enquiring minds with a generous amount of leisure time in which to pursue their personal hobbies and interests. The most celebrated of these was Gilbert White of Selborne, the great naturalist, but many other parsons also exercised their talents on various aspects of local history. Some dug into ancient burial mounds with great enthusiasm while others spent long hours seeking written history in old documents, for which their familiarity with Latin could make them particularly suited.

Rev J C Blomfield was one of this latter group. He came from an ecclesiastical family – an uncle being Bishop of London[8] and his father rector of Launton from 1837 to 1842. His own appointment to Launton dated from 1850 when he was 29 years old. So far as residents of Cottisford were concerned, his appointment to a Parish seven miles away (11 km) probably did not create much of a stir at the time, but it eventually proved very significant. J C Blomfield clearly had a keen interest in local history and must have explored archives far and wide relating to this part of north Oxfordshire.

He served as rector of Launton for no less than 45 years, for most of that period being Rural Dean. More than thirty years after his appointment he started publishing a series of scholarly volumes which remain today standard works on the history of the area. The first of these[9], which appeared in 1882, was entitled "A history of the present Deanery of Bicester" and over the next 12 years a further eight volumes appeared under his authorship.

The second volume[10], published in 1884, described the history of the Town and Priory of Bicester and the third volume[11], published in 1887, described the history of Cottisford and the neighbouring Parish of Hardwick with Tusmore. This volume was dedicated to the Earl of Effingham, who lived at Tusmore House. The history of a further 15 Parishes in the Bicester

Deanery was recounted in the remaining six volumes.

The opening pages of Blomfield's description of Cottisford in his third volume derived from early records following the Norman Conquest in 1066 when the Parish, like many others in England, was given as a reward to one of William's henchmen. It soon passed into the ownership of the Abbey of Bec in Normandy.

The French records of Bec Abbey seem not to have survived and most of the buildings there, other than fragmentary foundations, have long since disappeared. The only substantial surviving building is a major tower (fig. 1, page 54) on which a large plaque (fig. 2) records the fact that several early Archbishops of Canterbury and Bishops of Rochester originated from Bec.

Fortunately for the historian, many records of the English properties of Bec Abbey still exist and Rev Blomfield extracted from them a considerable amount of information about the Parish in the 12th to 14th Centuries.

In 1404 Bec's ownership of Cottisford was terminated by King Henry IV. After a succession of noble owners it passed in 1441 to Eton College, newly founded by King Henry VI. From that time onwards the surviving records increase considerably, and Rev Blomfield was able to extract details of leases and other matters relating to the Parish right up to his time of writing.

170 years before Blomfield's history of the Parish was published, another historian of note – Richard Rawlinson – visited Cottisford and took notes for a projected History of Oxfordshire upon which he had embarked. Sadly, he never completed the project, but his notebooks[12] survive in the Bodleian Library and provide various snippets of information about the Parish in the early 18th Century.

Readers seeking a reasonably brief, but authoritative, summary of the early history of the Parish could do no better than turn to the much more recent account in the Victoria County History (VCH). This unique project, started in 1899 with the Queen as its first patron, moves on slowly and further volumes are published at irregular intervals. Cottisford was covered in Volume 6 for Oxfordshire[13] which appeared in 1959.

The VCH account of Cottisford[14] corrects a significant mistake made by Blomfield. On page 8 of his History he asserts that "the village, the church and the chief estate of Cotesford ... find no mention ... in the Domesday Survey of 1086". He was evidently misled by the fact that

Figure 2

Figure 3

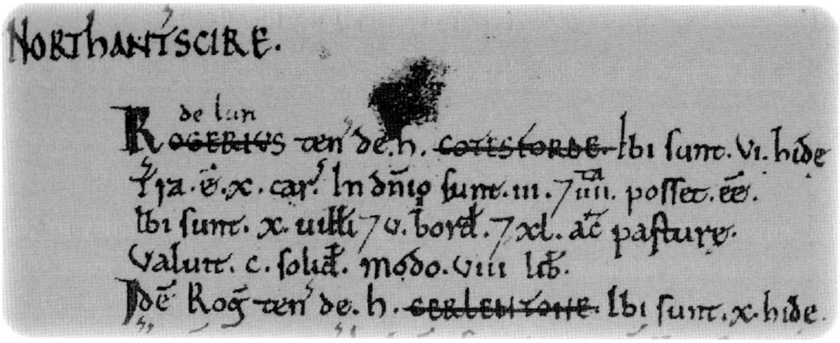

Figure 4

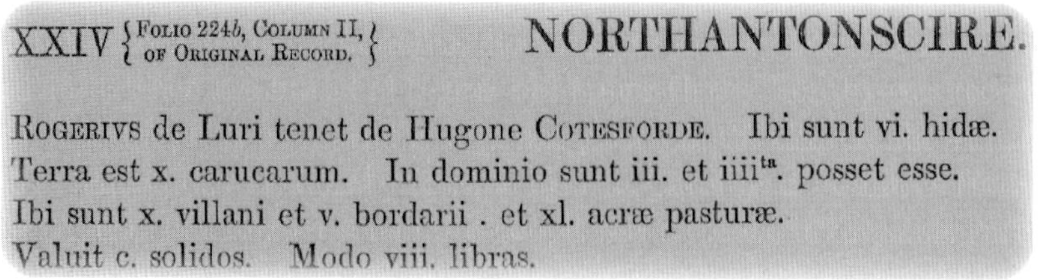

Figure 5

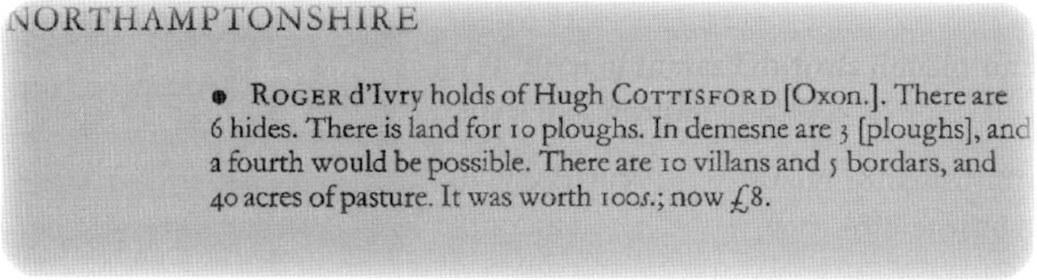

Cottisford did not appear in the survey where it might have been expected, under the section covering the County of Oxfordshire, but instead in the section covering Northamptonshire. The same is true of three other Parishes – Charlton-on-Otmoor, Shipton on Cherwell and Sibford Gower – which were also then, as now, situated in Oxfordshire. According to Volume 1 of the VCH[15] this was probably because all four Parishes were then held by Roger of Ivry and in the possession of Hugh of Grantmesnil who held extensive lands in Northamptonshire. At all events, the 1086 survey provides a first, very brief, account of the Parish as it was in Norman times. A facsimile of the original entry is reproduced here (fig. 3), together with a Latin transcript (fig. 4) and an English translation (fig. 5).

It is said of the Domesday Survey[16] that "the population figures recorded are probably households (ie one villein is really one villein and his household) except in the case of slaves and clergy who are probably individuals. It is usual to employ a multiplier to obtain some indication of total population of a Domesday manor; perhaps 4 or 5 for each head of household". On this basis, the 10 villeins and 5 bordars recorded in Cottisford in 1086 suggest a total population of 60 to 75 in the 11th Century. Which is about half the population of the Parish today, ten centuries later[17n].

3. THE LORD FAMILY – THE YEARS OF ABUNDANCE

The surname "Lord" was not uncommon in north Oxfordshire in the 17th Century, but Cottisford Parish Registers contain only one entry of the name before the end of that century – a baptism in 1693 which does not appear to have been connected with the abundance which soon followed.

In the nearby Parish of Fritwell, however, the baptism had taken place in February 1664 of a four-day-old infant, Lawrence Lord (2), the son of Lawrence Lord (1) and Anne his wife. This couple had six further children – five daughters and another son – baptised at Fritwell from 1669 to 1682. From 1673 onwards the father of these children was invariably referred to in Fritwell Parish Registers as "Mr Lord", indicating that he was a person of some substance. Later, when Lawrence Lord (2) matriculated at Exeter College, Oxford in 1683 his father was referred to[18] as "Gent".

In 1675 Lawrence Lord (1) took on from Eton College the lease of their estate in Cottisford and Fringford. The annual rent was 17 guineas plus 22 quarters of best wheat and six quarters and three bushels of malt, or the price thereof. This rental, made up of a combination of money and produce, had been required under an Act of Parliament[19] dating from Queen Elizabeth's reign designed to protect colleges from inflation of the currency. There was, in addition, a substantial renewal charge to be paid (in money) every seven years. Although there was a clause in the lease requiring Lawrence Lord (1) to live in Cottisford, preferably in Cottisford House (then known as Barsis Place), there is no evidence that he actually moved from Fritwell. Subsequent renewals of the lease in 1682, 1686, 1693 and 1700 invariably referred to him as being "of Fritwell".

In his Will (made in November 1702) he referred to himself as "Lawrence Lord the elder of Fritwell" and when he died (in 1708) he was buried at Fritwell. He then also had property in the Parishes of Souldern and Little Tew, which he left to his younger son, Robert. All his surviving children, except his eldest son, received significant legacies ranging up to £700. The eldest son, Lawrence Lord (2), received no such legacy or any property, but the sum of twenty shillings under the terms of the Will "to buy him a ring and no more in regard I have given so liberally to him already".

It seems probable that by the time Lawrence Lord (1) made his Will his elder son Lawrence Lord (2) was married and living at Cottisford House. At all events, less than a year later – in August

Children of Lawrence Lord (2) and his wife Anne	
Elizabeth	bapt 1703 died 1703
Lawrence (3)	bapt 1705 died 1743
Anne	bapt 1706 died 1774
Allen	bapt 1707 died 1771
William	bapt 1708 died 1712
Edward	bapt 1710 died 1713
Robert	bapt 1711 died 1744
Elizabeth	bapt 1712 died 1712
John	bapt 1713 died 1772
Mary	bapt 1715 died 1726
Eliza	bapt 1716 died 1793
Sarah	bapt 1718 died 1785
Lydia	bapt 1719 died 1720
Alicia	bapt 1721 died 1781
Lydia	bapt 1722 died 1783
Matthew	bapt 1724 died 1724

1703 – the first baptism of a child of Lawrence Lord (2) was recorded at Cottisford. Thereafter, over a span of just under 21 years, fifteen further children were born to him and his wife Anne, the last being baptised in August 1724. As can be seen from the list on the previous page, all sixteen baptisms related to single births. The intervals between the baptisms averaged just over 18 months and ranged down to as little as 11 months.

The first of these babies (named Elizabeth) died after only a few days in August 1703. In December 1712 two more of the children, aged 9 months and 5 years respectively, died within a few days of each other, one of them again having been named Elizabeth. All three of these early deaths were commemorated (in Latin) on a small memorial tablet in the floor of St Mary's church on the north side of the chancel (fig. 6). Four of the subsequent children also died young, at ages of a few days, 6 months, 3 years and 11 years respectively. With the relatively rudimentary state of both medicine and hygiene in those times, such early sadnesses were not unusual. Indeed, the fact that more than half the children survived into adult life (nine out of sixteen) may well have been better-than-average.

In many ways Lawrence Lord (2) appears to have been a typical country gentleman of his time. He was a Justice of the Peace – the records of Quarter Sessions at Michaelmas 1713 showing him adjudicating when William Topping of Cottisford and Richard Smith of Finmere were charged with assaulting Silvester Wellicomb. In 1700 he was recorded[20] as having five undertenants living in the Parish. He was also a man of wide interests, subscribing to erudite publications[21] such as "The British History, translated … from the Latin of Jeffrey of Monmouth" dated 1718. One of his sons, Robert, followed in his father's footsteps by matriculating[22] at Exeter College, Oxford while another son, John, matriculated at Hart Hall, Oxford and Lawrence Lord (3) matriculated at Trinity College, Oxford.

Lawrence Lord (2) evidently lived in some style at Cottisford House, his Will of 1727 mentioning a "chariot", which he left to his wife together with the "best pair of mares". His eldest son Lawrence Lord (3) received the furniture of his best room at Cottisford while his second son, Allen, received his watch and "which of my riding mares that he shall choose".

He had also prospered. At the renewal of his lease by Eton College in 1707 he was said to have rebuilt Cottisford House, which was then described as "a good house". By 1711 he evidently owned lands near the River Thames at Pidnells in Chipping Farringdon (Berkshire). In

Figure 6

Figure 7

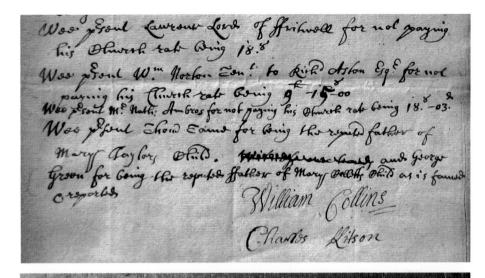

Figure 8

that year his name appeared in a varied list of transgressors (fig. 7) when the Churchwardens of Farringdon recorded "Wee present Lawrence Lord of Fritwell for not paying his Church rate being 18 s(hillings)".

By the time he came to draw up his Will in 1727 his estate also included Trenley Park in Kent and lands in the nearby Parish of Souldern (recently purchased from his brother Robert, senior), in addition to the Manor of Cottisford and Fringford. Such scattered holdings may seem surprising at a time when cross-country travel was uncertain and time-consuming – the property in Kent lay east of Canterbury and over 100 miles (160 km) from Cottisford. Even more unexpected is the fact that Lawrence Lord (2) also owned substantial property in the Parish of Kemys Inferior (Monmouthshire), held the Advowson there (the right to appoint a priest to the Parish church) and was at one time Sheriff[23] of that county.

Lawrence Lord (2) was 63 years of age when he died in 1727, as recorded (in Latin) on his memorial stone on the chancel floor in St Mary's church. Although his marriage has not yet been traced, it is clear from their ages at death that his wife Anne must have been about 20 years his junior. Her memorial alongside his, dating from 1772, although now considerably worn by the passage of innumerable feet, records that she was the relict of Lawrence Lord Esq by whom "she had issue 17 children" (fig. 8). The figure 17 appears clearly enough on the memorial but is one more than the number of baptisms recorded in Cottisford Parish Registers. It also seems to be confirmed by the Latin inscription[24n] on his memorial slab alongside: besides the four sons and five daughters who survived him, this refers to "eight other issue which his wife bore him". Perhaps there was one other child of their union which was baptised elsewhere. Alternatively, they could perhaps be forgiven if they had lost count.

At all events, whether the number of babies was 16 or 17, all that childbearing apparently did not seriously affect Anne Lord's health. Her memorial records that she died in her 89th year, having been a widow for 45 years.

The eldest surviving son, Lawrence Lord (3), died (apparently intestate) in 1743 at the relatively early age of 38 and was buried at Cottisford, though no memorial to him survives. The youngest two of his three surviving brothers had both gone into the church. One of them, Robert, having obtained a BA at Oxford in 1731 and an MA at St John's College, Cambridge in 1736 was then for a short time Curate at Kemys. But in 1738 he was appointed Curate of the Parishes of Chetwode and Barton Hartshorn, in Buckinghamshire only four miles (7 km) from Cottisford. He died young, apparently unmarried, in 1744 and was buried at Buckingham[25n].

The other brother who entered the church – John Lord – obtained his BA at Hart Hall, Oxford in 1735 and his MA there in 1738. He eventually became Rector of Kemys, but lived at one stage in Chipping Norton and died locally at Culworth in 1772. At Sulgrave a memorial in the church (fig. 9) commemorates both him and his wife Anna. She was the daughter of a clergyman, Moses Hodges, who had inherited the Manor and Manor House at Sulgrave.

The second oldest brother in this generation, Allen Lord, did not go into the church but moved to Kemys where he married a local girl, Temperance Blethyn, and eventually became Sheriff of Monmouthshire[26] like his father before him.

After the death of Lawrence Lord (3) the family ceased to live at Cottisford House. His eldest surviving sister, Anne, had already married Rev Shuckburgh Cotton at Cottisford in 1732, but his four other surviving sisters and his widowed mother moved from Cottisford to Culworth in Northamptonshire nine miles (14 km) away. Two of the sisters married at Culworth, Sarah to Richard Bartholomew in 1748 and Alicia to John Somerscales in 1751.

The whole family clearly retained strong links with Cottisford. On the deaths of the

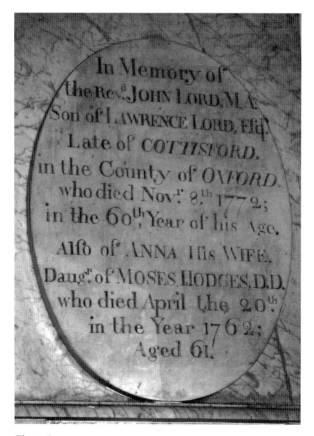

Figure 9

matriach, Anne, in September 1772 and the two unmarried daughters, Lydia in January 1783 and Eliza in March 1793, they were brought to Cottisford for burial in the vault under the floor of the chancel in St Mary's church, where two large stone slabs commemorate them and record their links with Lawrence Lord (2). Several of these deaths were recorded in Jackson's Oxford Journal, invariably referring to their links with Cottisford, as shown below (figs. 10–13).

Last week died at Culworth, in Northampton-shire, in the 99th year of her age, Mrs. Lord, relict of Lawrence Lord, Esq; formerly Lord of the Manor of Cotisford, in this county.

On Sunday died of a dropsy, at Culworth, in Northamptonshire; the Rev. John Lord, M. A. formerly of Cottisford, in this county.

Last Tuesday died, at Burford, in this County, Mrs. Bartholomew of Woodstock, Wife of Mr. Alderman Bartholomew of that Borough, and one of the Daughters of Lawrence Lord, Esq. formerly of Cottesford in this County.

Last Saturday died, Mrs. Somerscales, Relict of the Reverend Joseph Somerscales, M. A. of Emlode, in Worcestershire, and one of the Daughters of Lawrence Lord, formerly of Cottesford, in this County. And a few Weeks ago departed this Life, her only Son, the Reverend William Somerscales, M. A. late of Balliol College, in this University.

Figures 10–13

4. THE LORD FAMILY – THE WELSH CONNECTION

The Lord family's estate at Kemys Inferior, in south Wales, was not just another scattered piece of land in their ownership which would generate useful rent. Despite its distance from Cottisford – 80 miles (130 km), which even today involves an awkward cross-country journey – this estate became home for several members of the Lord family. The mammoth "History of Monmouthshire" published by Sir Joseph Bradney in 1923 included[27] "pedigrees" of "the family of Lord of Cottisford and Kemeys", and also of their descendants "the families of Cotton and Risley". Bradney also transcribed[28] four memorials in Kemys church, which recorded the burial there of eight members of the Lord family.

The Manor of Kemys Inferior had been owned by the family of Kemys for hundreds of years until, as recorded by Bradney, "George Kemeys served the office of Sheriff in 1699, and about 1700 sold his manor and advowson of Kemeys to Laurence Lord of Cottesford in Oxfordshire". Despite the mention of Cottisford in this sentence it seems likely that Lawrence Lord (1) of Fritwell actually initiated this purchase. It probably formed part of what he said in his Will he had "given so liberally" to his eldest son Lawrence Lord (2). The likelihood of this is increased by the fact that one of the first members of the family to be buried in Kemys church was one of Lawrence Lord (1)'s generation, his only brother Robert who died there in 1744.

Lawrence Lord (2) was Sheriff of Monmouthshire in 1719 and one cannot help wondering whether his repeatedly pregnant wife had to accompany him on the journey there when he undertook official duties. When he died in 1727 the first bequest in his Will was to his wife "£200 that she may be able to stock Kemeys demeasnes being part of her jointure" – the provision defined for a widow in the marriage settlement. This suggests that ownership of the property at Kemys may have been initiated by his marriage to Anne.

Three of Lawrence Lord (2)'s sons were associated with Kemys in one way or another. As mentioned in the previous chapter, John Lord was Rector there shortly before his death in 1772 and Robert Lord was Curate there in 1732. But the son of Lawrence Lord (2) most involved with Kemys was Allen Lord who married, Temperance, the daughter of Timothy Blethyn in about 1736. They had three children baptised at Kemys and presumably lived there. When Allen Lord died at the age of 64 in 1771 he was buried in Kemys church where a flat slab in

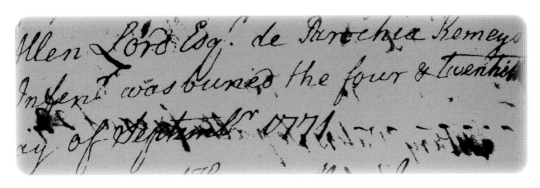

Figure 14

the north aisle commemorated him, as described by Bradney. The relevant entry in the Parish Register is shown in figure 14. Sadly, the church was swept away[29n] in the 1960s to allow the construction of the dual carriageway A449 below the Manor of Kemys Inferior.

The Manor House survives today on the steep hillside overlooking the valley of the River Usk five miles (8 km) from Newport, as pictured in figure 15. During the 18th Century the Lord family owned other lands in the vicinity, including parts of the Parishes of Llantrisant and Cwmyoy, as mentioned in the Will of Lawrence Lord (2). It was not until the 20th century that the family's link with Kemys was finally severed.

Figure 15

5. THE LORD FAMILY –
A THIRD OF A THIRD OF A FIFTH

In 1728 Lawrence Lord (2) "breathed his last with four sons and five daughters surviving him", as recorded on his memorial in the chancel floor of Cottisford Church[30]. At a time when having male heirs was of great importance to those with real estate to pass on, the survival of four sons aged from 15 to 23 must have seemed reassuring. But it was not to be.

The eldest of these sons – Lawrence Lord (3) – inherited the bulk of his father's real estate, being situated at Kemys in Wales, at Chipping Farringdon in Berkshire and at Trenley Park in Kent, together with the estate at Cottisford leased from Eton College. However, the second son, Allen Lord, inherited another piece of real estate, 80 acres in Souldern, which Lawrence Lord (2) had purchased from his brother, Robert senior, not long before making his Will in 1727.

When Lawrence Lord (3) died young and intestate in July 1743 he evidently had no heirs and his affairs were dealt with by his unmarried sister Eliza. As a result of the fortunate survival of copies of many of the family's papers[31n] in a solicitor's office in Buckingham, it is still possible to follow the descent of the separate parts of Lawrence Lord (2)'s original real estate. Lawrence Lord (3) had already relinquished the lease on Cottisford House before he died: under the terms of his father's will the property in Wales descended to his eldest surviving brother, Allen.

In February of the following year, another of the brothers, Robert Lord, also died young and apparently without heirs, as recorded in Chapter 3. This left two sons of Lawrence Lord (2) remaining. Both lived longer and married, but neither of them had any sons. Allen Lord, who died at Kemys in 1771 at the age of 64, had three daughters, of whom two survived him. John Lord married when he was 31 a woman of 43, who bore him no children.

The total lack of male heirs in this generation of the Lord family had quite different results on the subsequent ownership of the two estates at Kemys and Souldern. The Kemys estate in Monmouthshire passed down[32] through Allen Lord to his two daughters, Eliza Davies (formerly Lord) and Temperance Lord. Neither left issue and both passed their interest in the Kemys estate to their cousin Rev Holford Cotton, Rector of Kemys and Vicar of Adderbury. He died without issue in 1822 and from him the estate passed to his niece Sarah Ann Risley. And from her eventually to her grandson, Rev William Cotton Risley, Rector of Shalstone, who sold the Estate, Manor and Advowson of Kemys in 1906 for the sum of £14,750. After more than 200 years in the ownership initially of Lawrence Lord (2) and then of his descendants, the Kemys estate thus, in the end, enjoyed single ownership.

By contrast, ownership of the Souldern lands[33n] first became divided when John Lord, the last surviving son of Lawrence Lord (2), died in 1772 – he left it equally to his five surviving sisters. Two of these sisters were then, and remained, unmarried. When the first of these two, Lydia Lord, died in 1785 she left her share of the Souldern lands to her sister Eliza Lord. When Eliza died in 1793 her two-fifths of the estate was divided under her will: one third to one niece; another third equally to two other nieces; and the remaining third equally to three more nieces. The three married sisters all had children to whom their shares eventually descended, and further subdivision followed in the next generation. When the estate was finally sold (for £2,300) in 1825 the distribution of the cash generated was recorded[34] by the Buckingham solicitors on a calculation sheet (fig. 16).

The arithmetic was complicated by the fact that when Allen Lord died in 1771 he had been considerably in debt to his mother. A bond of £700 existed which had passed on to Eliza Lord and which now had first to be repaid, divided into two one-third shares and three one-ninth shares.

In addition to this calculation sheet there is also in existence a letter[35] from one of the lesser beneficiaries, Mr Heynes, to the solicitor Mr Hearne in which he complained that the statement of his share, £193-6s-7 ¾d, was "much under the value". Mr Heynes suggested that "from the complicated nature of the many different rights in the Estate some error from misinformation may have taken place in the division". Despite these critical comments, he concluded his letter with "united regards to Mrs Hearne".

It was in the Buckingham office of this solicitor, Thomas Hearne, that the substantial archive of documents relating to the Lord family's lands at Souldern survived over many years. The most informative document is a large draft "Abstract of Title to the several Parts and Shares of an Estate at Souldern in the County of Oxford (formerly Lord's)" referred to in Reference 33n above. This provides detailed information tracing ownership from 1702 through to 1827 and was evidently drawn up when the eventual owner of the Souldern lands, John Risley, wished to raise a mortgage of £300 on them. The whole document of 46 large folios was clearly prepared with great care after a very considerable amount of painstaking research – perhaps not unrelated to the fact that it was from the solicitor himself, Thomas Hearne, that John Risley wished to borrow the money!

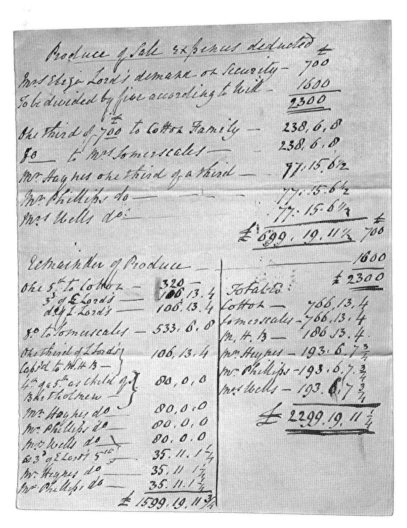

Figure 16

6. A TROUBLED COURTSHIP

In the village of Marsh Gibbon, about five miles (8 km) south-west of Cottisford and just over the county boundary into Buckinghamshire, is a long-established farmhouse known as Westbury Manor Farm, Here, in 1994, a remarkable discovery was made.

Workmen carrying out renovations upstairs in one of the bedrooms removed some floorboards and came across four tightly folded pieces of paper beneath the floor. When these were unfolded and examined they proved to be letters of a very personal nature which had remained unseen for more than 270 years. They had evidently been folded up small and hidden by slipping them through the gaps between the floorboards

Transcripts of the four letters appeared in the 1994 Annual Report of the Buckinghamshire Record Office. They dated from 1723 and were of two very different kinds. Three of them were written to a girl by an ardent suitor who swore undying love and his firm intention to make her his bride - "while life & breath remains I will be yours & only yours" (fig. 17). The fourth was from the girl's mother, exasperated that her daughter had been meeting and corresponding with this man and warning her, in the most dramatic terms, of his total unsuitability as a potential husband. He was evidently a minister of the church, but according to the writer he had on one occasion been so drunk that he could not read prayers. The mother forecast dire consequences that would follow if she married him – "... my thinks I see thy Children run about bare foot and bare leged for it can be nothing but begary insue ..." (fig. 18).

The discovery of these letters raised several intriguing questions. First and foremost, by whom and to whom were they written? There was little difficulty in identifying the suitor – he had signed all three of the letters, with his name, John Wells, preceded by closing greetings which became progressively more passionate with each letter, the third concluding: "I am my Dear, Yor Ever Constant, Faithfull, Fond, & Loving Spouse, till Death, Jn° Wells" (fig. 19).

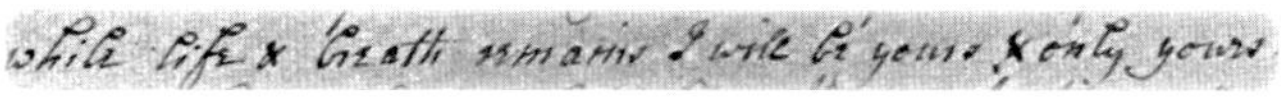
while life & breath remains I will be yours & only yours

Figure 17

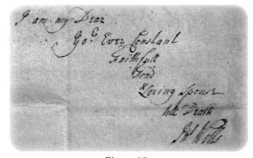

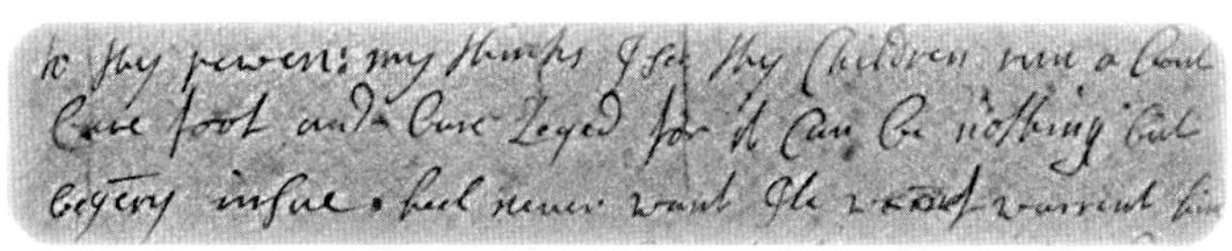
to thy parents; my thinks I see thy Children run a bout
bare foot and bare leged for it can be nothing but
begary insue.

Figure 18

I am my Dear
Yor Ever Constant
Faithfull
Fond
& Loving Spouse
till Death
Jno Wells

Figure 19

He was readily identified as the third child of John and Elizabeth Wells, who had been baptised at Cottisford in September 1685. He had taken holy orders[36] after obtaining his BA at Exeter College, Oxford, in 1705, and by July 1723 – when the letters were written – was Vicar of Caversfield and also Curate of Barton Hartshorn cum Chetwode, three miles (5 km) north of Westbury Manor Farm. At that time Caversfield, although close to Bicester, was a detached Parish of Buckinghamshire and thus in the same county as Barton Hartshorn cum Chetwode.

The identities of the mother and daughter were at first more difficult to establish. John Wells had addressed his first two letters to "My dearest Dear" and the third to "My Dearest Dear Jewell", providing no clue as to the girl's name. And both he and the girl's angry mother had abbreviated several personal names in their letters. The mother had started her letter with the phrase "Ld I have not patience till I se you …" (fig. 20) and had signed herself off as "LG". Within the letter she had referred to John Wells' mother as "Old Bess", but two other people had been referred to only as "A L" and "A T".

After the letters had been deposited at Buckinghamshire Record Office the staff there carried out detailed, wide-ranging research to identify the mother and daughter. It was eventually shown beyond doubt that the mother was Lydia Guy (1), a younger sister of Lawrence Lord (2) of Cottisford. She had married Sam Guy of Bledington, a village 20 miles (32 km) WSW of Cottisford, just over the county border into Gloucestershire, in 1687. The marriage had taken place by licence, when she was 18, with the consent of her father, Lawrence Lord (1) of Fritwell. In his Will, made in 1702, Lawrence Lord (1) stated that "Whereas I have already advanced my daughter Lydia in Marriage with whom I have given a good Fortune I do hereby give to her three children Lydia Samuel and William Guy the summe of Ten pounds a piece to be paid to them when they come to the Age of One and Twenty …" (fig. 21). Although no record of the baptism of Lydia Guy (2) has been found, this Will conclusively shows that the recipient of the four letters was his granddaughter, a niece of Lawrence Lord (2) of Cottisford.

Further details gradually emerged. Westbury Manor Farm was at that time the property of the Townsend family. In 1709 John Townsend, then a widower and Lord of the Manor of Westbury, had married Mary Lord, a sister of Lydia (1): the marriage had taken place at Chetwode and was performed by John Wells, Curate. It is clear from the letters that in 1723 Lydia (2) was

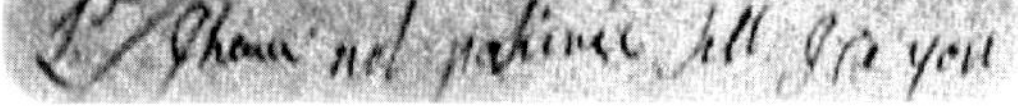
Ld I have not patience till I se you

Figure 20

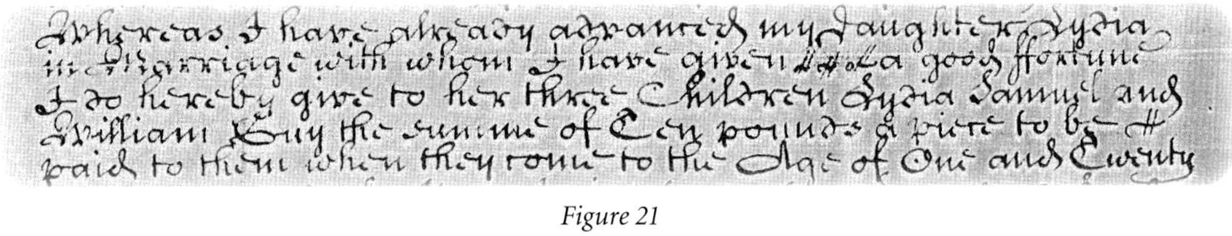
Whereas I have already advanced my daughter Lydia
in Marriage with whom I have given a good ffortune
I do hereby give to her three Children Lydia Samuel and
William Guy the summe of Ten pounds a piece to be
paid to them when they come to the Age of One and Twenty

Figure 21

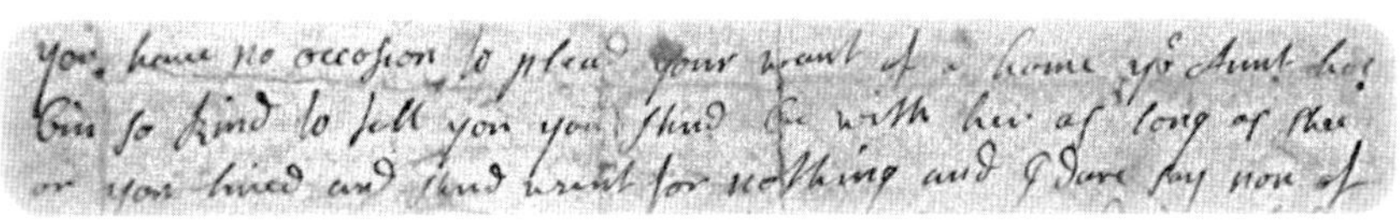
You have no occasion to plead your want of a home yr Aunt has
been so kind to tell you you should be with her as long as she
or you lived and should want for nothing and I dare say none of

Figure 22

Figure 23

living with her aunt, by now widowed, and her mother made the point in her letter that "… you have no occasion to plead your want of a home y^{or} Aunt has bin so kind to tell you you shud be with her as long as shee or you lived and shud want for nothing …" (fig. 22).

Considerable local detail also emerged from the letters. On one occasion John Wells had stayed at Marsh (Gibbon) overnight and the following day had walked to Edgcott. He intended to go to Fritwell Feast – provided his beloved was also to be there. His widespread ecclesiastical responsibilities at the three churches in Caversfield, Barton Hartshorn and Chetwode were presumably facilitated by the fact, referred to in his third letter, that he owned a horse.

The Lord family of Cottisford clearly took an interest in the dispute. In his first letter John Wells bemoaned the possibility that the two of them might be banished one another's company. And in his second letter he wrote (fig. 23) "My Dear I would not have y^{ee} concerned about my going into Wales, for I am not certain thereof; it is true your AL (presumably Aunt Lord) asked me whether I would accept of Kemys, if vacant at Michaelmas" – Kemys being the Parish in Monmouthshire of which Lawrence Lord (2) held the advowson. If this happened, John Wells assured the girl that he would not be there above a month in the whole year.

Apart from the virulent opposition of the girl's mother, John Wells also faced the need to earn more money. Indeed, one cannot help wondering whether the mother's views were coloured by the fact that he was the son of a yeoman, a distinctly lower class in the social scale than the monied Lord and Guy families. In his first letter he had written that "… when I am in a capacity of maintaining you like a Gentlewoman, I will marry you …".

Figure 24

True love eventually triumphed two years after the letters had been written, when John Wells was appointed Rector of Siston near Bristol, and married Lydia Guy by licence at Stoke Lyne in September 1725.

It would be nice to be able to record that they lived happily ever after but, as so often happened in those times, their marriage was brief and saddened by early deaths[37n]. Their first child, named John, was born in June 1726 but died when only nine months old in March 1727. In September of that year another son was born to them, also named John, and in January 1729 Lydia produced twin girls named Lydia and Elizabeth. But within seven months Lydia and her two baby daughters were all dead. The first of the twins, Elizabeth, died in May 1729 and the two Lydias, mother and daughter, died within two weeks of each other in July 1729.

In the chancel of Siston church (fig. 24) is a brass plaque (fig. 25), recording in Latin the burial of Lydia and of the three children all within a year of their birth. John Wells was left a widower with a young son less than two years old, and remarried the following year. He maintained his connection with the Lord family of Cottisford, being appointed Rector of Kemys in 1732, though he also continued as Rector of Siston until his death in 1753 at the age of 68.

Little can young Lydia have imagined, when she slipped those four tightly folded letters between the floorboards, that the sad little tale of her troubled courtship would be brought to light so many years in the future. We must be grateful that she hid them, because their survival allows us a brief, but fascinating, glimpse of her personal life in those far-off times. And reminds us that basic human problems remain much the same from generation to generation.

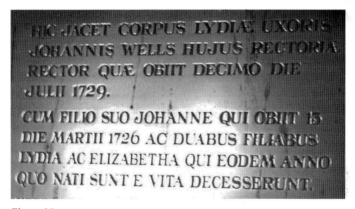

Figure 25

7. AN 18TH CENTURY FUNERAL

In addition to burials in the vault under the chancel of Cottisford Church, descendants of one branch of the Lord family continued to be buried in the churchyard for many years after the matriarch, Anne, and the surviving unmarried members of the family had removed to Culworth.

Immediately outside the east end of the church, close to the chancel, are seven large "ledger" stones commemorating eight of these descendants. Such stones, initially flush with the ground, tend over the years to become covered, first with moss and then gradually with turf. Their outlines can often still be discerned because of the moss, and this must have been the case in 1989 when the late William Bell drew a plan of the churchyard and on it showed seven dotted outlines there. During the "Spring Clean" of the churchyard in 2002 the concealing turf was peeled back from these stones and their inscriptions became visible for the first time in many years (fig. 26). Although some of the stones were badly cracked, the wording of the inscriptions on them proved to have been preserved in good condition.

These ledger stones commemorate members of the Cotton family. Anne, the eldest surviving daughter of Lawrence Lord (2), who had been born at Cottisford House in 1706, married here in 1732 Rev Shuckburgh Cotton, who was then Rector of Upper Heyford. Their first child was baptised here in 1733 but after Shuckburgh had also been appointed Rector of Newton Purcell at the end of 1734 they moved there and their eight further babies were all baptised at Newton Purcell.

Figure 26

Living only three miles (5 km) from Cottisford, this family evidently maintained close ties with the Parish. Three of their children died young and were buried here, though their graves are unmarked today. When Rev Shuckburgh Cotton died in 1762 he was buried here and commemorated on the first of the ledger stones. Anne and five of her six children who lived into adulthood were also buried here, all except one of them being commemorated[38] on further ledger stones. The last of them, Rev Charles Cotton was buried in 1799.

Rev George James Sale, the husband of her only married daughter, Lydia, was

Children of Rev Shuckburgh Cotton and his wife Anne (formerly Lord)	
Holford	bapt 1733 died 1740
Charles	bapt 1736 died 1799
Anne	bapt 1739 died 1768
Elizabeth	bapt 1741 died 1795
Mary	bapt 1743 died 1798
Lydia	bapt 1744 died 1787
Holford	bapt 1746 died 1822
Alicia	bapt 1749 died 1749
Shuckburgh	bapt 1750 died 1750

also buried here and commemorated on a ledger stone. A detailed commentary on these ledger stones will be found in Appendix D.

Surviving documents from the office of Solicitor Thomas Hearne of Buckingham (already referred to in Chapter 5) include a series of accounts relating to the household of Charles Cotton, clerk, during the years 1795 to 1799. These accounts allow us some fascinating glimpses of the last few years of Rev Cotton's life, and also provide a very detailed picture of his funeral at Cottisford, as well as the funerals of his two unmarried sisters Elizabeth and Mary a few years earlier. Rev Charles Cotton died in September 1799, as recorded in a short obituary notice in Jackson's Oxford Journal (fig. 27). Like his father he had been Rector of Upper Heyford, but he lived at Tingewick, in Tingewick House on Upper Street.

He evidently lived there in some style. His wine merchant's accounts[39] show that during the final 18 months of his life he was supplied with two dozen bottles of Sherry, five dozen bottles of Lisbon, one dozen bottles of Old Port and one dozen bottles of Madeira, together with substantial quantities of Brandy, Raisin Wine and Beer. An inventory[40] taken shortly after his death shows that his possessions included a large amount of mahogany furniture, including a reading desk, a writing desk, a Pembroke table, a tea table, a sideboard and no fewer than four dining tables, one oval and three square, two of the latter having leaves. The "linnen" included 26 pairs of sheets: the cellar contained two casks of 1½ hogsheads each, three half-hogshead casks and one small cask: the silver included a Punch Ladle weighing 23oz 15dwts: and the outbuildings included Brew House, Dairy, Shoe House, Coal House and Coach House & Stable. The whole of Rev Cotton's effects were valued by one John Day at £244-8s-0d.

On Wednesday the 20th instant died at Tingewick, in the county of Bucks, after a very severe and lingering illness, which he endured with truly christian patience and resignation, the Rev. Charles Cotton, formerly Fellow of New College, and Rector of Upper Heyford, in this county.—An affectionate parent, an indulgent master, and a warm friend.

Figure 27

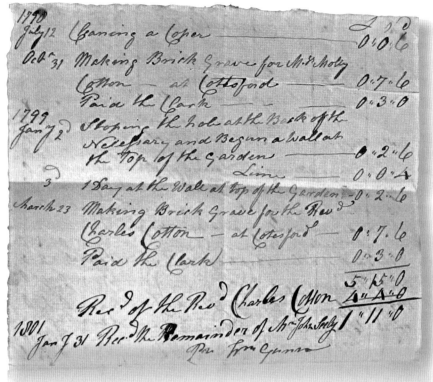

Figure 28

At intervals over the years, Rev Charles Cotton had employed a handyman by the name of William Gunn to carry out miscellaneous jobs in and around the house. The costs were carefully recorded in an account[41] covering a period of 4½ years. Amongst many items indoors, he repaired a grate in November 1795 (1s-0d) and in September 1797 cleaned two coppers (1s-0d). Out of doors, in May 1797 he made a drain from the dairy (5s-10d) and in January 1799 stopped up the hole at the back of the "necessary" and began a wall at the Top of the Garden (2s-6d). This latter item is shown in the short excerpt reproduced here (fig. 28).

On three occasions during this period Willam Gunn was sent over to Cottisford to prepare for the burial of a member of the family. On the first occasion, in January 1795, when Rev Cotton's sister Elizabeth died, William Gunn spent "3 days Making Brick grave for Mrs Elizabeth Cotton at Cotesford (7s-6d)", "Paid the Clerk for Labour and Cleaning the Church (3s-8d)" and "Paid for care of Horses (2d)". On the second occasion, in October 1798, William Gunn made a further brick grave at "Cottsford (7s-6d)" for "Mrs Molly Cotton" (Mary). This time he paid the Clerk 3s-0d but there was no mention of cleaning the church. The third occasion, in March 1799, was to make the "Brick Grave for the Revd Charles Cotton at Cotesford (7s-6d)" and again to pay the Clerk (3s-0d). Both of these last two items are shown on the excerpt above.

Another surviving account[42] (fig. 29) from one Thomas Harvey shows two coffins being provided, the first in October 1798 for Miss Mary Cotton (£3-12s-0d) and the second in March 1799 for Revd Mr Cotton (£3-15s-0d).

Several other accounts for these funerals survive, all from Philip and Thomas Box, who evidently fulfilled the role known today as undertakers. One of these accounts[43] totalling £13-18s-9d relates to the funeral of Miss Cotton in October 1798. Two accounts[44] relating to the funeral in March 1799 of Revd Charles Cotton comprise 36 items costing a total of £29-12s-0d and provide particularly full information about that funeral: copies of both these accounts are reproduced in Appendix C, together with transcripts.

Rev Charles Cotton's coffin was covered with black cloth and inside was lined with white crepe (£1-15s-0d). A "Man's superfine suit and pillow" were provided (£1-15s-0d). The conveyance of the coffin from Tingewick to Cottisford involved a hearse and four horses provided for the day (£2-12s-6d) with a coachman and postilion (5s-6d), both of whom were wearing "black cloaks" (5s-0d) and provided with ribbon to tie hatbands (1s-2d). The return journey along a section of the Buckingham to Banbury road involved a Turnpike cost of 1s-2d and the Parish Clerk at Cottisford was paid a further 5s-0d.

Messrs Box provided a wide range of clothing and accessories for mourners at Rev Cotton's funeral. These included 4 silk hatbands (£2-2s-0d), 3 silk scarves (£2-15s-0d), 30 yards of crepe for 15 hatbands (£3-0s-0d), 8 pairs of men's black loops (18s-0d), 8 pairs of men's grey beavers (16s-0d), 10 pairs of women's grey beavers (£1-0s-0d), 3 pairs of men's black silk (gloves) (15s-0d), 1 pair of women's ditto (5s-0d) and 1 pair of ditto extra long (7s-0d). Also supplied were substantial quantities of various materials, including velveteen, cotton, muslin, shammy skins, Holland and Bombazine, together with Epaulets, silk pockets and breast plates.

Such ostentatious and expensive funerals in a quiet country churchyard must surely have been unusual occasions in the life of the Parish. For humbler burials, few of the mourners will have been able to afford special clothing and the body will have been conveyed to the church on a simple bier: the footpath from Juniper Hill to Cottisford across the fields is said to have been wider than usual and known as a "bier path". And in most cases there will have been no durable memorial to mark the last resting place of the deceased. Apart from the seven ledger stones commemorating Anne Lord's family there are today only five surviving 18th Century memorials in the churchyard, although more than 190 interments were recorded as taking place here during that Century.

What the local residents, many of whom must have been grindingly poor, thought of such lavish funerals as that of Rev Charles Cotton can only be conjectured today. But one cannot help wondering whether the memory lingered on in the Parish. 44 years later, when squire James Edwards Rousby of Cottisford House made his Will he directed, by contrast, that "… my funeral be conducted in a decent frugal manner …"

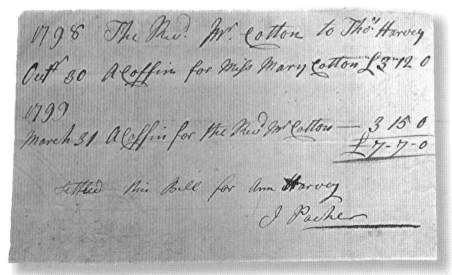

Figure 29

8. A VERY DIFFERENT LORD OF THE MANOR – RICHARD EYRE

In 1739 Cottisford Manor was leased by Eton College to Richard Eyre of the East India Company. This was a very different type of lessee, having no obvious previous connections with the locality, but being a junior member of a distinguished Wiltshire family His father is recorded as having been Prependary of Salisbury and his nephew Chief Justice of the Common Pleas[45].

Richard Eyre retired to Cottisford in 1741 at the age of about 42, after many years of service with the East India Company. His life as a country gentleman in this quiet corner of north-east Oxfordshire must have been very different from his previous experience in India. Fortunately, voluminous and detailed records of the East India Company have survived and can be consulted today amongst the India Office Records at the British Library. These documents provide a remarkable glimpse of the activities of both the Company and its employees. A few excerpts will illustrate something of the long-vanished world in which Richard Eyre had spent most of his life before settling in Cottisford.

He started his service with the East India Company in 1715 as a "writer" (a junior employee) at the age of about 16. In March of that year the manifest[46] of the ship "King George" sailing to India included a "chest of apparel Freight Free" for the use of Mr Richard Eyre, writer, during the voyage (fig. 30). The Company employed several others of the same surname in the early years of the 18th Century, including Sir Charles Eyre (Governor of Fort William in Bengal, 1695–1701), Robert Eyre (Merchant), Christopher Eyre (Merchant) and John Eyre ("Chief" in 1715–1718). It has not been established whether these were relatives, but it seems very likely as the name is not particularly common.

Richard Eyre served at several of the Company's "factories" in Bengal including Calcutta and Patna, but the surviving records of him relate mainly to his final years of service when he attained the post of "Chief" of the factory at Cossimbazar[47n]. This trading post on the River Ganges about 120 miles (190 km) above Calcutta disappeared long ago, but was for many years one of the most important factories of the East India Company. First established in 1658, it was said[48] in 1676 to "send abroad every year two and twenty thousand bales of silk every bale weighing a hundred pounds" – i.e. almost a thousand tons of silk annually.

Richard Eyre's appointment as Chief of Cossimbazar was recorded[49] in November 1738. The Factory was a substantial place, the grounds and buildings having been valued[50] earlier in the century at more than £23,000. A payroll for the month after Richard Eyre's arrival there[51] as Chief, December 1738 , shows that more than 230 Indians were employed at the factory, all working 7 days a week. A year later the number of Indian employees had increased to 370.

The main business was the purchase and processing of silk and other materials from dozens of local suppliers for shipment to England. The Company seems also to have been engaged[52]

> MR RICHD. EYRE WRITER
>
> 1 CHEST OF APPARREL FREIGHT. FREE BEING FOR HIS OWN USE IN THE VOYAGE.

Figure 30

in bringing substantial quantities of saltpetre (used in making gunpowder) from Patna down the river to Calcutta.

The number of British merchants and writers was less than a dozen. But there was also a significant military force at Cossimbazar. On Richard Eyre's arrival[53] this comprised a Lieutenant, a Brevet Ensign, a Master at Arms, 4 Sergeants, 2 Corporals, 3 Drummers, 36 Privates and a Gunner. At Calcutta, the Company's main base in Bengal, this force was backed up by another Master at Arms having a substantial armoury[54] including a variety of field pieces, more than 12,000 "Iron Shott" of various sizes, and gunpowder valued at more than £2,000.

Such military forces safeguarded the Company's interests in a variety of ways. In 1740 a Sergeant and 9 men were sent[55] to take charge of a "Petre boat to Calcutta" and on another occasion the President and Council instructed[56] Cossimbazar that a complainant was to be sent to Calcutta "under a strong guard of soldiers".

Occasionally the Company's military forces were involved in punitive expeditions. Richard Eyre will doubtless have followed with interest the news of dramatic events at the Company's base in Madras in November 1721 following the wrecking of the "King George", the ship in which he had travelled to India six years earlier. The "King George" had been lying offshore on 13th November ready to depart for England, when there was a great storm[57] during which "rains and floods carried away most of the poor people's houses in the Suburbs of Madrass". When the weather cleared there was no sign of the "King George" offshore and reports soon came in that the ship had been driven ashore and "broke to pieces". There were also reports of "some Goods driven ashore" and of four white men dead.

A mariner attempting on 19th November to engage in salvage of the Company's goods heard that "the Moors seem inclinable to mischeif" and it soon became clear that they had "carry'd 11 men and some bales up the Country". Three boats, each containing an officer and seven soldiers, were sent to investigate but one of them was oversett "by which misfortune a Serjeant and three men were drowned". A warning was sent by the Company that it would "certainly make reprizals" if any of the Company's Goods were retained. This warning was ignored and it was reported that "the Moors are removeing the men and Bales higher into the Country". A few days later "All gentle means having failed for the recovery of the Men and Bales from the King George's Wreck" Lieutenant Sutherland was ordered "to use force if the Moors would not comply". This he did. His party marched against a place called Chyore where they freed the prisoners and were "necessitated to attack Dindar Cawn" the ringleader, who, "together with severall others were burn'd in a house where all the Bales were". Having themselves taken 10 prisoners, the party then put the deserted town to the torch.

Such warlike diversions were fortunately rare, and Richard Eyre's duties as Chief of Cossimbazar were primarily commercial. When he took over the post from one Mr Halsey the latter delivered over to him[58] "the Cash Books of Accounts Merchants Contracts and all other Papers in his Possession belonging to the Honble Company", together with full details of "the balance of the books".

Detailed Minutes were kept of meetings (known as "Consultations") and of correspondence with the Board in Calcutta, most of which survive today in the British Library. These records show how sensitive the Company was to possible competition. Trading posts in Bengal were also operated by the Dutch, with whom reasonably cordial relations seem to have been maintained, but when ships from other countries appeared every possible obstacle was placed in their way. In 1730 an "Ostend" ship was captured[59] after three of her crew had been wounded by a shot and the Dutch were informed of its large cargo. The Ostenders protested loudly, but to no effect. In 1738 a Swedish ship was expected to arrive in Bengal and detailed instructions were given[60] to ensure that she received no assistance or trade of any sort.

In April 1739 there was apprehension of possible difficulties with a new local Nabob, but by June the Board had agreed[61] that the Prime Minister, Hodjee Hamid, "a great favourite of the new Nabob" should be paid a sweetener of 10,000 Rupees.

Surviving books of accounts provide many personal details, such as the £28-14s-6d paid[62] to Richard Eyre in 1739 for his expenses in travelling from Calcutta to Cossimbazar. A larger sum was recorded[63] a few months later for the hire of a boat to convey the Company's bales from Tillingay to Calcutta, the "boat which came from Patna being broke".

These books also give an illuminating glimpse of trading conditions – debts being divided[64] into three separate categories, headed "Good Debts", "Doubtfull Debts" and "Desperate Debts", the last two headings being illustrated in figure 31.

It has been said[65] of the Company's servants in the early eighteenth century that they generally "remained in India until they had accumulated enough wealth to retire to England". Apart from their service on behalf of the Company, many of them indulged in business on their own account. Richard Eyre eventually overstepped the mark in this connection.

The Board in Calcutta always kept a watchful eye on the operations of its various factories and in 1740 the President and Council became concerned about the quality of the silk from Cossimbazar "being very bad this year". Towards the end of the year Richard Eyre was required[66] to go down to Calcutta to be examined about this poor quality. One explanation put forward was "the fighting between two armies". This did not satisfy the Board and

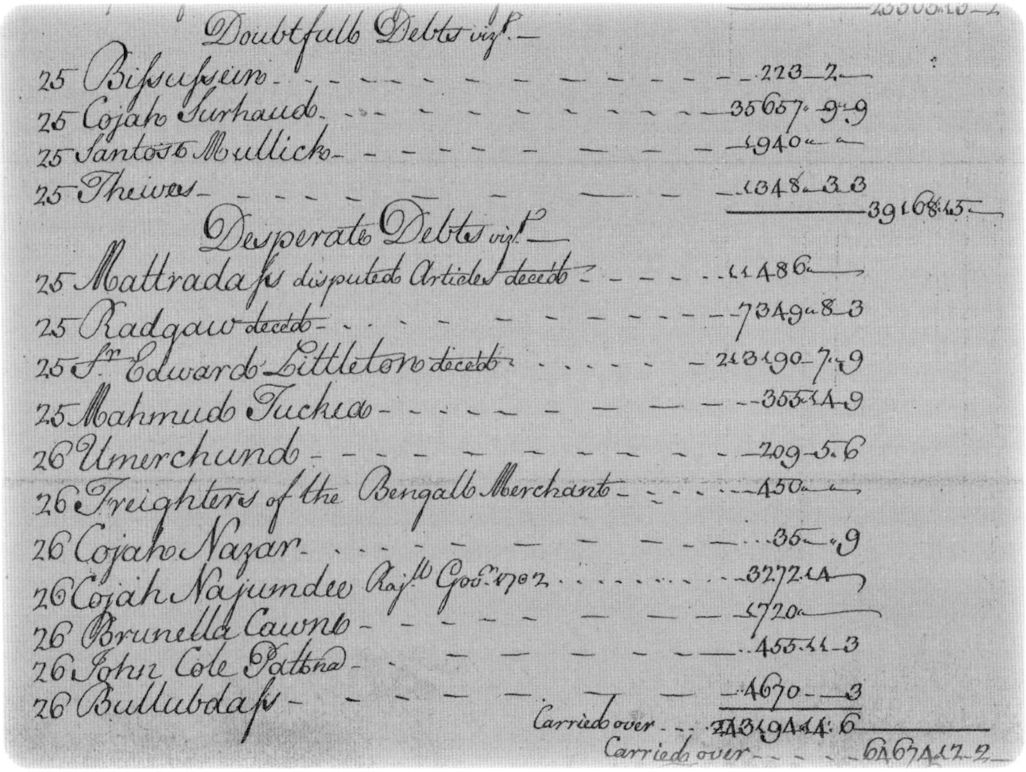

Doubtfull Debts viz.t

25	Bissussein	223–2–	
25	Cojah Surhaud	35657·9·9	
25	Santoss Mullick	1940	
25	Theivas	1348·3·3	39168·15–

Desperate Debts viz.t

25	Mattradass disputed Articles deceds	11486
25	Radgaw deceds	7349·8·3
25	Sr. Edward Littleton deceds	213190·7·9
25	Mahmud Tuckeas	35514·9
26	Umerchund	209·5·6
26	Freighters of the Bengall Merchant	450
26	Cojah Nazar	35·9
26	Cojah Najumdee Rajll Gov.r 1702	32721·4
26	Brunella Cawns	1720
26	John Cole Pathna	45511·3
26	Bullubdass	4670–3
	Carried over	243194414·6
	Carried over	643417·2

Figure 31

subsequently four members of his staff and five native merchants were similarly required to go to from Cossimbazar to Calcutta to be examined. Two of the former, Messrs Kemp and Eyles, made written statements.

In December 1740, after further discussions[67] in Cossimbazar, Richard Eyre wrote an affidavit stating that several of the merchants had alleged that "they were loasers by my private silk last year" and detailing the prices he had paid for various items of silk in April and May 1739. He added that he could later have contracted at a lower price, but refused. This document was signed by Richard Eyre and the four members of his staff who witnessed that he "did swear on the Holy Evangelists to the truth of the above written in Council".

The dispute between the Board in Calcutta and the factory in Cossimbazar clearly centred on Richard Eyre's private trade and was further complicated early in 1741 when the written statements of Messrs Kemp and Eyles were "absolutely denied" by the native merchants[68].

This resulted in more documents being sworn on oath. Eventually, in February 1741, the Board brought the matter to an untidy close by writing a letter[69] to the factory at Cossimazar where the following was recorded: "As Mr Eyre had made Oath his private trade had not been either directly or indirectly in any ways detrimental to the Honble Company's investments to the best of his knowledge ... as there was no proof appeared of any frauds having been committed in providing the raw silk they had directed Mr Eyre to return to the duty of his Station as Chief of this factory and strictly charge us to take the utmost care that nothing of the like kind happen in future ...", the latter part of this message being reproduced in figure 32.

This rebuke was soon followed, in March 1741, by a letter[70] from the President and Council advising that they had appointed Sir Francis Russell as Chief of the Cossimbazar factory. Richard Eyre was ordered to deliver over the charge of the factory to Sir Francis on his arrival, which he duly did in April, handing over the balance of cash and one of the keys to the treasury.

Richard Eyre's dispute with the Company's Bengal headquarters was not an isolated incident, nor even particularly unusual. The fact that "Chiefs" of factories (and even lesser employees) were permitted to carry on private business in the identical commodities they were purchasing on behalf of the Company inevitably led to conflicts of interest and disputes. Despite his disagreement with the local Board in Calcutta, he appears to have stayed on in India for the rest of 1741, it being recorded[71] that he "reached the post of Accomptant and Member of Council by the time of his retirement in December 1741".

Though young men like Richard Eyre employed by the Company in India had the prospect of quickly becoming reasonably wealthy, they also faced the possibility of discomfort, disease and early death in hot and insanitary conditions. Sir Francis Russell, the man who succeeded Richard Eyre as Chief of the factory at Cossimbazar in April 1741, was indisposed[72] in February

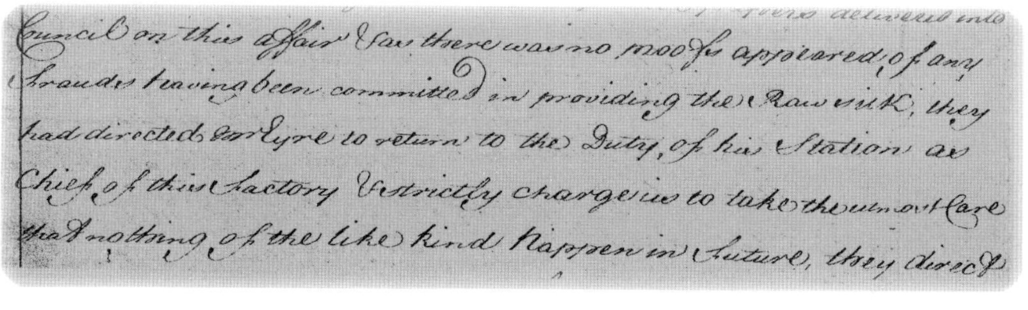
Council on this affair & as there was no proofs appeared of any
frauds having been committed in providing the Raw silk, they
had directed Mr Eyre to return to the Duty of his Station as
Chief of this Factory & strictly charge us to take the utmost Care
that nothing of the like kind happen in Future, they direct

Figure 32

1742 and dead by the following month[73]. In Richard Eyre's own family, his younger sister Elizabeth had been granted permission by the Company[74] in October 1728 "to go to her brother Richard in Bengal". Less than two years later, in February 1730 she married one William Barwell (who many years later became Governor of Fort William there). But Elizabeth died childless in September 1731 and a monument to her in the churchyard of St Johns, Calcutta recorded that she was in her 22nd year.

Several published accounts of life in the Company's factories in Bengal show that travel[75] was generally undertaken by water, along the River Ganges and its tributaries, with all the uncertainties and risks that that involved. But there was also at Cossimbazar a high-quality "Pallakeen" – known usually today as a palanquin – the pole-mounted litter in which a fortunate individual (often European) could make journeys on land in relative comfort, being carried by four or six native bearers while shaded from the burning rays of the sun. The Pallakeen at Cossimbazar was valued[76] at no less than £350, and must have been an impressive sight, having "Silver Plate feet and Tassels".

Presumably this particular Pallakeen was used only on special occasions, but it must have seemed a very distant memory to Richard Eyre after he had taken up residence in Cottisford House. The Oxfordshire natives hereabouts will doubtless have doffed their caps or curtsied, as appropriate, but he is unlikely to have enjoyed anything like the degree of subservience he had experienced so recently in India[77n].

British employees of the East India Company do not appear ever to have returned home on leave, even when serving in India for several decades: the voyage under sail round the Cape of Good Hope would have taken several months in each direction. It would accordingly be intriguing to know how Richard Eyre decided to take on the lease of Cottisford House in 1739, three years before returning to Britain. It was a major step and, if he had never seen the place, must have seemed a considerable gamble.

No evidence has been found of Richard Eyre having been married while in India. But six years after his return to Britain, on 20th September 1748, he married Martha Clitherow by licence[78] at Hanwell, Middlesex. The name of Clitherow had been a notable one in the early history of the East India Company, Sir Christopher Clitherow having accommodated the headquarters of the Company in his premises in the City of London for ten years in the 17th Century, and the couple may possibly have met through that connection.

Writing in 1888, more than 100 years after the death of Richard Eyre, Blomfield recorded that "during his eighteen years of residence at Cottisford he was a power in the village life, and even after his death it was long before he was forgotten. These were the days of popular superstitions, and many stories are current, even yet, recalling some feature of his life known to the villagers – eg that he was seen driving his four-in-hand &c; that he was buried in a cask in a pond &c".

Although retired into the countryside he evidently kept in touch with national affairs, in 1747 paying the postmaster[79] at Buckingham 17s-9d annual subscription for a newspaper, probably the London Evening Post. He will doubtless have been shocked when the news came through of the disastrous events in Bengal in 1756, culminating in what has since been popularly known as "The Black Hole of Calcutta". One of those who died there[80] was Edward Eyre, said to be a brother of the Dean of Wells and also of Robert Eyre, formerly Chief of the Company's factory at Patna, as shown in figure 33. He may well have been related to Richard.

Martha was about 39 years of age when they married and does not appear to have had any children. When Richard died in 1761 his Will was short and simple, leaving all his real and personal estate to "my dear wife Martha" and making her his sole Executrix. A fine marble memorial on the south wall of the nave in Cottisford church, erected by his widow, refers to his long service with the East India Company and his having been Chief of their factory at Cossimbazar.

> ### EYRE, EDWARD
>
> *Tenth of Council. Store-keeper and Military Store-keeper. Arrived Calcutta, 16th October 1741. He had been married, as the Parish Register records the birth of a daughter, Jane Mary, 24th January 1754, who died 17th June 1755, but whether his wife was living or not is uncertain. Died in the Black Hole.   The French account, 3rd July 1756, says he died next day. Grose says he was brother to the Dean of Wells and to Mr. Robert Eyre, formerly Chief of Patna*

Though much remains on record of her husband's long service with the East India Company, relatively little has been discovered about the life of Martha Eyre. She is also commemorated in Cottisford Church, a neatly matching further section having been added later at the foot of her husband's memorial (fig. 34).

Her Will, made a year before her death in 1772, is an interesting document, providing several glimpses of the way in which Cottisford House was furnished at that time.

The bulk of her considerable estate went to relatives, who included such notables as a nephew – James Eyre – who was Recorder of the City of London, and another nephew, Mr Justice Blackstone[81n]. A sum of £3,000 was left to the children of her late brother and several Godchildren also benefited.

Figure 33

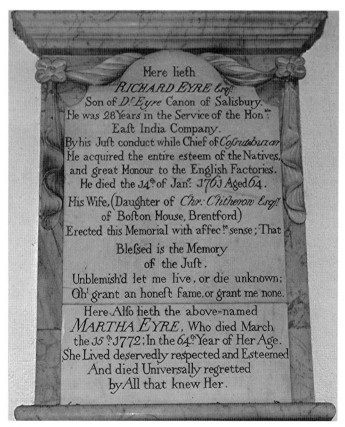

Figure 34

Two Trustees were appointed, one from Bibury and the other from Westminster. For their accommodation and convenience, and for facilitating sales as directed, Cottisford House was to be reserved and continued for six months after her decease, with all servants willing to continue residing there. Her faithful servant Catherine Palin was to receive £200 and all her wearing apparel, old and new, and a niece of Catherine was to receive £50. Her servant Richard Dutton was to receive £100 and the choice of any one of her saddle horses.

Family pictures hanging in divers rooms in Cottisford House included portraits of her late husband, Richard Eyre; his mother and father Eyre; and Lady Pembroke: all these pictures were left to James Eyre. Her amboyna wood writing desk, her gold watch and her pebble tweezer set went to various Goddaughters. Her servant Catherine Palin also received two chests, one described as "the Large India Chest", and Richard Dutton also received her "weather glass now hanging in my parlour".

Every one of her cottage tenants in Cottisford Parish whose rent did not exceed 30 shillings per annum received a legacy of 50 shillings. And each day labouring man who had worked one year employed in her service in or about her farming business received 5 shillings.

The advertisement for sale in Jackson's Oxford Journal 6 months after her death (fig. 35), gives additional detail such as "Damask Beds and Window curtains … Turkey and other Carpets, Japanned Cabinets, Plate …" and "a large Quantity of Linnen".

Martha directed that she should be buried in the same grave as her "dear husband in the Church of Cotisford". Which effectively scotches the local superstition, mentioned by Blomfield, that he had been buried in a cask in a pond.

TO be SOLD by AUCTION,
By Mr. BARFORD,
On the Premises, by Order of the Executors of Mrs. MARTHA EYRE, deceased, on Tuesday the 29th of this Instant, and the two following Days; —— All the neat and genuine Houshould Furniture, Side-board of Plate, Linnen, China, &c. at the Manor-House of Cotsford, near Bicester, Oxfordshire; the Whole consisting of Damask Beds and Window curtains, Mahogany Chairs and Tables, Pier-Glasses, Turkey and other Carpets, Japanned Cabinets, Plate, a large Quantity of Linnen, a small Library of Books, good Kitchen Furniture, and various other Articles.—To be viewed on Saturday the 26th Instant, to the Time of Sale, which will begin each Day punctually at Twelve o'Clock.
CATALOGUES may be had five Days before the Sale, at the principal Inns at Bicester, Brackley, Buckingham, the Place of Sale, and at Mr. Barford's, in Piccadilly, London.
N. B. Some Time in the Month of January next will be sold by Auction, by Mr. BARFORD, at his Great Room in Piccadilly, London, The Manor-House of Cotsford, with the Lands thereunto belonging. In the mean Time the Premisses may be seen, by applying to Mr. Dutton, at the Manor-House aforesaid.

Figure 35

9. THE HOUSE OF TEBBY

The surname Tebby is not particularly common in Oxfordshire, but the Parish Registers of Cottisford contain nearly 100 entries of that name over a period of more than 200 years from 1679 to 1890. The record is remarkably continuous and allows six generations of the family living in Cottisford to be traced through changing times. The first generation, Jacob Tebby and his wife Mary, had lived through the Civil War and the Commonwealth: the sixth generation ended with Henry Tebby who found a brief mention in Flora Thompson's "Lark Rise" and lived on into the 20th Century.

The history of these six generations illustrates the remarkable continuity of family life in rural areas at that time, with the majority of individuals spending all their lives in one Parish or its immediate neighbourhood. Although the Tebbys were not particularly distinguished, and most of them were probably not well off, one of their number did play a significant part in the development of Juniper Hill, and the family deserves a place in any record of the Parish.

It is not clear where Jacob Tebby and his wife originated. The first record of the surname in Cottisford was the baptism of their son John in 1679 and a further five of their children, all sons, were baptised in the years up to 1698. Three of these sons eventually married and settled down in the Parish. The eldest of the three, Richard, had seven children. The youngest of the three, Samuel, had three daughters, and the next senior, James Tebby born in 1695, had two sons. The "tree" overleaf (fig. 36), extracted from the Baptism Register, outlines the development of these and succeeding generations of Tebby in Cottisford.

It was John Tebby, baptised in 1711, the eldest son of Richard Tebby, who evidently played a key role in the creation of the new settlement at Juniper Hill. A note in the Parish Registers records that in 1754 two cottages were built at Juniper Hill for the use of the poor of the Parish. At that time the whole of the north-western part of the Parish was uncultivated heathland. Several tracks, which have long since disappeared, criss-crossed the area but there were no other dwellings nearer than "Woods House" (near the present pig unit) and "Knights House" (alongside the Turnpike – now the A43).

The cost of building the two cottages at Juniper Hill was recorded as being £28-7s-6d, met by seven landholders, the chief of whom were Richard Eyre Esq of Cottisford House and the Rector, Rev Smith. Amongst the other five names was that of John Tebby. He must have played more than a subsidiary role in this development because the surviving map[82] of Eton College's Cottisford Estate from the late Eighteenth Century shows only one building at Juniper Hill and it is labelled "Tebby's house" (figs. 37 and 38, pp. 50–53).

Apart from his involvement in the building of the first houses at Juniper Hill, this John Tebby also undertook official duties in the Parish. In 1757 he was a Churchwarden. And when a notice was published in Jackson's Oxford Journal in August 1769 (fig. 39) listing Collectors of Land and Window Tax who were still in arrears for 1766 his name appeared, as shown here. The sum involved was relatively small – 1s-6d – but all the Collectors were advised that if they did not pay the arrears to the Under Sheriff when he attended at the Star Inn, Oxford, on two successive Saturdays in September they would be distrained without further notice.

This John Tebby was buried here in 1795 at the relatively great age of 84. The fourth generation of Tebbys in the Parish was that of his cousin Richard, the younger son of James Tebby and Mary, who was born in 1732 and married Ann Chimes in 1759. Their union produced nine

TEBBY FAMILY BAPTISMS AT COTTISFORD

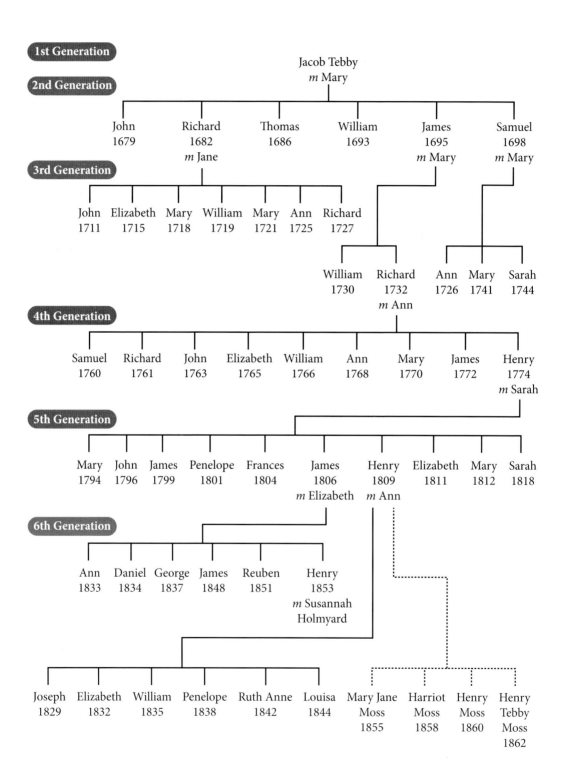

Figure 36

children, three daughters and six sons, the youngest of whom – Henry – eventually married Sarah Hodgkins at Mixbury and produced a family of ten children in the fifth generation. The summary of the 1801 Census, described in the next chapter, confirms correctly that in February of that year Henry Tebby was four in family, three males and one female. He had two surviving sons who had been baptised in 1796 and 1799, and their next child did not arrive until a month after the Census. Two of their sons, James baptised in 1806 and Henry baptised in 1809, eventually married and produced the sixth generation of Tebbys in the Parish.

The younger of the two brothers in the fifth generation who stayed in the Parish, Henry Tebby, did not follow in the footsteps of many of his forbears by becoming an agricultural labourer. In successive Censuses he was recorded as a higgler in 1851, a shepherd in 1861 and a gamekeeper in 1871.

He had also served a previous spell as gamekeeper, which nearly cost him his life. On the evening of 12th January 1845, while gamekeeper for J E Rousby of Cottisford House, he was sent on an errand to engage a man for work the following day. While passing a plantation near Hethe he heard the scream of a hare and, going to investigate, found three poachers. When he addressed one of them – John Jesse Willis – by name, he was attacked and savagely beaten about the head repeatedly with heavy hedge stakes.

After rendering Tebby insensible, the three men ran off. Eventually he came round and, although bleeding profusely, managed to make his way to the house of the Roman Catholic priest, Rev A Maguire. News of the attack was sent to Mr Rousby and medical assistance was called from Brackley. Willis was arrested that evening.

Two cases followed later that year at Oxford Assizes. John Jesse Willis of Hethe was indicted first and in the next session John Watts aged 22 and William Neale (also of Hethe) aged 19 were also charged with causing grievous bodily harm. The cases attracted wide publicity, being reported not only in Jackson's Oxford Journal but also in other provincial newspapers and The Times of London (fig. 40). At the second trial the judge, Lord Chief Justice Denman, commented on the enormity of the offences. All three men were sentenced to 15 years' transportation.

At the time of this attack Henry Tebby was 35 years of age. He had married Ann Cadd of Newton Purcell early in 1827, when he was only 18, and she had borne six children between 1829 and 1844. But she died in 1854 and his domestic arrangements then became less conventional.

Left by his wife's death with several children still to raise – the youngest of them 9 years of age – Henry not surprisingly engaged a housekeeper. She was a married woman by the name of Mary Ann Moss, who was 13 years his junior. In 1851 she had been living with her husband, Isaac Moss, and their three daughters less than ½ mile (0.8 km) from Juniper Hill at Knight's

PLOUGHLEY HUNDRED.

Ardley, Richard Young and Vin. Ring, junior,	0	1	6
Charlton upon Otmore, Richard Cooper and John Harris,	6	15	4
Cottesford, Richard Dutton and John Tebby,	0	1	6
Fencott and Mercott, Richard Howlett and James Pain,	4	11	5
Fringford, William Allum and William Fame,	0	0	10
Hampton Gay, Thomas Hindes, Clerk, and John Brooker,	2	19	5
Hampton Poil, Anthony Hedley and John Hitons,	3	0	7
Hardwick and Tusmore, Wm. Gamble and Sam. Knibbs,	0	10	0
Lower-Heyford, John Shears and Henry Mims,	0	4	2
Islip, John Young and John Smith,	11	10	10
Noke, William Purdie and Thomas Crauford,	0	1	8
Souldern, Thomas Bignall and John Smith,	0	11	4

Figure 39

Walesby addressed the jury for the prisoners. Lord Denman summed up, and the jury, after a short deliberation, returned a verdict of Guilty against both the prisoners. The learned Judge, in passing sentence, said that the prisoners had been convicted of one of the worst assaults he had ever heard of in a court of justice. It was most fortunate indeed for them that the dreadful injuries they had inflicted did not cause death, or they would then have stood at the bar capitally convicted. Though no fatal result had ensued, there could be no doubt that morally they were even now guilty of murder. It is, said his lordship, abominable that in this country men should think that a gamekeeper is a victim that a poacher may kill like a hare. This cannot be tolerated; it must be put a stop to. The statute was imperative, and he had no option, but the prisoners' friends might apply for mitigation of the punishment to another quarter. The learned judge then sentenced both the prisoners to fifteen years' transportation.

Figure 40

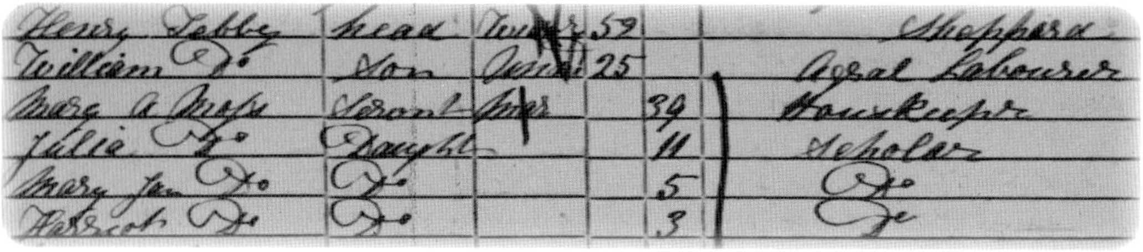

Henry Tebby	Head	Widr	59		Shepherd
William Do	Son	Unmd	25		Agrl Labourer
Mary A Moss	Servant	Mar		39	Housekeeper
Julia Do	Daughter			11	Scholar
Mary Jane Do	Do			5	Do
Harriot Do	Do			3	Do

Figure 41

House alongside the turnpike. When she moved into Henry Tebby's household she brought the youngest of these daughters, Julia Moss, with her. She soon started producing another family, four babies arriving from 1855 to 1862.

The Census excerpt in figure 41 illustrates the position in 1861 when Henry had living with him a son, William, by his marriage; Mary A Moss, shown as "Servant" and "Housekeeper"; a daughter, Julia, of her marriage; and two further daughters named Mary Jane Moss and Harriot Moss.

The Registration of births, which had been introduced in 1837, together with the available enumerators' returns from the various Censuses, reveal nothing as to the paternity of the four children born to Mary Ann Moss when she was Henry Tebby's housekeeper. On each of the four birth certificates the "Name and surname of father" was left blank. In every case the birth was registered by the mother who was described on the certificate as "Mary Ann Moss formerly Rouse". No record has been found of her husband, Isaac Moss, having died.

Similarly, the relevant entries in the Parish Register for the first three of the baptisms drew no attention to any irregularity. When Mary Jane Moss was baptised on Christmas day 1855 the register described her simply as being the daughter of "Mary married woman". Similarly, when Harriet Moss was baptised in 1858 she was described in the Register as daughter of Mary. When a short-lived third child, Henry Moss, appeared in 1860 he was described as the son of Mary. But when Mary Ann Moss produced a fourth child – another boy – in 1862 any lingering doubts as to the paternity of these children must surely have been removed by the second of his given names – he was baptised as Henry Tebby Moss – though once again he was described as the son of "Mary, married woman".

Many years later, when these two daughters of Mary Ann Moss married, they did not hesitate to give the name of their father, as required on their marriage certificates, as having been Henry Tebby. Mary Jane Moss did that in 1874 and Harriot Moss twice, in 1876 and after the death of her first husband on remarrying in 1890. "Be sure your sins will find you out" – a common cautionary saying during Victorian times – certainly applied in this instance. The polite fiction in the Census return for 1861 that Mary Moss was merely "housekeeper" to Henry Tebby was eventually exploded without recourse to anything so complicated as genetic fingerprinting.

The elder of the two sons in the fifth generation, James Tebby, made a Will in 1875 four years before his death – a very unusual step for an agricultural labourer at that time, most of them having precious little to pass on to their descendants. In this Will James left legacies of £17 each to two of his sons, James and Reuben, and the residue of his estate to his other son, Henry Tebby, who became his executor.

It was this Henry Tebby, born in 1853, who became the last of that surname recorded in the annals of the Parish. He was referred to by Flora Thompson in Chapter XI of "Lark Rise" as being the squire's head gardener and, after a long engagement, marrying the schoolteacher[83n] who had taught both Flora and her brother Edwin at Cottisford school.

The marriage between Henry Tebby, gardener, and Susannah Holmyard (Miss Holmes of the book) took place in 1885. Susannah was 7 years older than Henry. At the time of the Census in 1901 they were still living in Cottisford, but she died in 1910 and he was living on his own in Cottisford in 1911. Their union was childless and there has now been no entry of the surname Tebby in the Parish Registers for well over a century.

10. A RARE SURVIVAL – THE 1801 CENSUS

The decennial Censuses of the UK, first instituted by the government in 1801, provide a wealth of statistical information about the population during the last 200 years – its numbers, distribution, age structure, composition and employment. That must clearly have been the intention of William Pitt's government, and their foresight has provided reliable data on the many remarkable changes that have taken place as the total population has soared from 11.7 million in 1801 to 58.7 million in 2001.

From the start, the information has been written up in two stages. First, on a "schedule" by someone in each household showing details of everyone who slept there on the night of the census. Secondly, by literate "enumerators" who visited every property in their allotted areas during the week following the census night to collect the schedules – and doubtless to discuss uncertain points with householders, many of whom will have been illiterate at the earliest censuses. From the "household schedules" they then prepared their own "enumerators returns" showing for every household the names of each individual, relationship to head of household, age, married status, occupation, place of birth and so on. The completed "enumerators' returns" have then been gathered together by the national government and analysed to obtain the required statistical data.

After each of the first four Censuses (1801–1831) had been completed and their results analysed and published, the manuscript enumerators' returns containing all the details of individuals were destroyed. But from 1841 onwards an important change was made. The government decided that the enumerators' returns would not be destroyed, but retained in the public records on condition that they would be under a 100-year embargo so as to retain confidentiality. This proviso was no doubt introduced to encourage full information being divulged to the enumerators, who were required in some Censuses to record sensitive details such as whether individuals were deaf and dumb, lunatics, imbeciles or living in workhouses.

This change has been of great value to historians. Over the years the retained enumerators' returns for each Census from 1841 to 1901 have been released for public scrutiny under the 100-year rule: those for 1911 are also now available with some of the potentially sensitive details omitted. Their usefulness has often prompted regrets that the comparable documents for each of the early Censuses from 1801 to 1831 were destroyed. Cottisford is fortunate that a rare relic of the 1801 Census has survived.

Accompanying the Parish Registers is a loose piece of paper (fig. 42) listing the basic facts about the 23 families resident in the Parish on 1st February 1801. Though the Census was not taken until more than a month later, on 10th March 1801, this is clearly an early draft, listing the names of heads of households and the number in each family. It might be expected that this record would have been made by the Rector, Rev Greenhill, but the repeated misspelling of the word "famley" makes that less certain. At all events, Rev Greenhill led the field with the greatest "number in family" – nine.

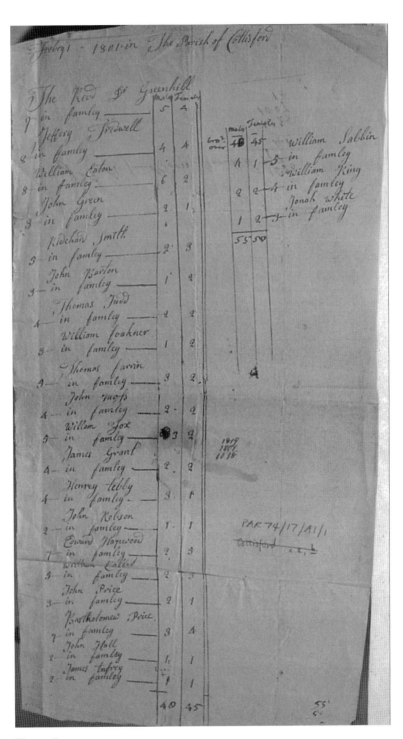

Figure 42

11. THE ROUSBY ERA
(FLORA THOMPSON'S SQUIRE BRACEWELL)

After a succession of relatively short-term occupants of Cottisford House, James Edwards Rousby took up the lease from Eton College in 1842. He and his eldest son were actually in residence there a year earlier at the time of the national Census in June 1841. Thus began a period of 87 years during which three generations of the Rousby family occupied the property almost continuously[84n].

The surname Rousby is, and has been for many centuries, relatively rare, originating principally in Yorkshire and neighbouring counties. It seems not to have been recorded at all in Oxfordshire until 1818, when the burial of 5-year-old James Henry Rousby was recorded in the nearby Parish of Souldern. A memorial to him was placed in the church, showing him to have been the son of James Edwards Rousby Esq and his wife Caroline of Souldern House. The following year the baptism of a further son of this couple was recorded in the same Parish and their address was again given as Souldern House. This, together with the use of the term Esq, shows that James Edwards Rousby was a person of some substance.

This branch of the Rousby family had come to Oxfordshire from the London area. Their marriage had taken place in St Albans Abbey in 1812, and the 5-year-old son who died at Souldern in 1818 had been baptised in Marylebone. Two other children had been born before the family moved to Souldern, and altogether six children of James Edwards and Caroline Rousby were baptised there in the years up to 1827. The reason for their eventual move to Cottisford House may well have been a need for larger premises and grounds[85n].

Children of James Edwards Rousby and his wife Caroline

James Henry	bapt 1813 died 1818
Caroline	born 1815 died 1842
Emily	bapt 1817 died 1880
Edwards	bapt 1819 died 1875
Henry	bapt 1820 died 1899
Arthur	bapt 1822 died 1863
Charles James	bapt 1823 died 1905
Helen	bapt 1825 died 1853
Lucy	bapt 1827 died 1906

Several surviving items of written evidence show that James Edwards Rousby was a forceful character. The first is a note in the Parish Registers of Souldern complaining of irregularities concerning the baptisms of the two youngest Rousby children, Ellen (or Helen) and Lucy. The Curate, J Cotton Risley, recorded in March 1828 that the parents had "neglected to send the names of the Children tho' repeatedly pressed to do so". These two children had apparently then been baptised by the vicar of Aynho and Newbottle – to whom "no blame attaches itself". The Curate procured "the names at last from the servants".

This may, perhaps, just have been due to a clash of personalities with the Curate. But of more significance was the Will that James Edwards Rousby made in 1843, in which he disinherited three of his seven surviving children. The reason is not spelt out in the Will, but his annoyance is clear enough.

Having referred to a sum of ten thousand pounds held by two trustees for the ultimate benefit of the children of the marriage, the Will then rehearsed the fact that since the death of his wife earlier in 1843 he was at liberty – alone – to direct in what shares and proportions the children should benefit:

> *"And whereas my said sons Henry and Arthur Rousby and my daughter Emily Rousby have acted in a manner unbecoming of my regard and having by their misconduct forfeited all claim to my consideration I do expressly declare it to be my intention to exclude them altogether from any participation not only in the said sum of ten thousand pounds but in any part of my property …"*

This was a drastic step, likely to affect adversely the career prospects of Henry[86n] (then aged 23) and Arthur (then aged 22), and the marriage prospects of Emily (then aged 26). It seems possible that there may also have been a rift between James Edwards Rousby and his wife, Caroline. The family had apparently maintained a toehold in Marylebone, where their first child had been baptised. On the day of the 1841 Census, when James Edwards Rousby was recorded at Cottisford House with their eldest surviving son, his wife was recorded in Marylebone together with their eldest daughter, also called Caroline, then aged 26. And it was in Marylebone that both daughter Caroline and mother Caroline died, in 1842 and 1843 respectively, the latter after a three-year illness.

It may also be relevant that James Edwards Rousby made his Will six weeks after his wife Caroline had died. Until her death he was not free, by himself, to disinherit any of their off-spring from participation in the sum of ten thousand pounds which had constituted the marriage settlement in 1812 and was held in trust for their children. During her lifetime Caroline would have had a say in how it should eventually be distributed amongst them.

That there had been a serious rift in the family is beyond doubt, and it was not mended during James Edwards Rousby's lifetime He did not die until five years after making the Will disinheriting Henry, Arthur and Emily, but he never altered it.

Happily, there is later evidence to show that relationships between the younger generation were not permanently fractured. Two years after her father's death Emily, the eldest of the disinherited children, was married at Cottisford and the witnesses included both of her surviving sisters and her eldest brother, Edwards. Emily also returned to Cottisford – with her husband – for the marriage of her sister Lucy in 1858, to which she and her eldest brother were witnesses: the ceremony was performed by another of the disinherited children, Henry, by then a Minister. And when Henry himself was married at King's Cliffe the following year Emily was a witness and her husband Gregory Bateman took the service. Lucy was with her sister Helen when she died in 1853 and attended the wedding of her brother Edwards in Devon in 1854.

James Edwards Rousby died in 1848. He was buried in Cottisford church, where he is commemorated in the chancel, both on a large stone slab in the floor and on a memorial on the north wall.

As was the custom amongst reasonably well-off families at that time, by far the greatest part of his estate passed to his eldest son, Edwards Rousby (born 1819), who inherited all the contents of Cottisford House, horses, carriages etc. On his marriage he was also to receive all the money in trust, subject to the payment of a £100 annuity to his youngest brother, Charles James, and £50 annuities to his sisters Helen and Lucy. In the event of Edwards Rousby dying without having married the whole benefit was to pass to Charles James Rousby. In the event of his also dying unmarried the whole benefit was not to pass to either of the two unfavoured sons but to a nephew, James Kendall, subject to his taking the surname Rousby.

Apart from bequests of £50 each to two of his servants, James Baines and Mary Bowerman, James Edwards Rousby also left £50 for his Executors to distribute at their discretion "amongst such of the poor of the Parish of Cottisford as may be my tenants at my decease". But he added a proviso – that those living "on the Heath of that part of my estate called Juniper Hill may not derive any benefit from this bequest". This again suggests that James Edwards Rousby was a forceful character. His exclusion of the inhabitants of Juniper Hill from any benefit under his Will probably resulted from their strong and sustained opposition to the enclosure of Cottisford Heath – a change that was then again in prospect.

With Edwards Rousby having inherited the family home, the other six surviving children of James Edwards Rousby tended to become scattered far and wide. Helen (born 1825) was single when she died at Bromley in 1853, but the other five all married.

Henry Rousby (born 1820), the elder of the two disinherited sons, had matriculated at Lincoln College Oxford in 1839 at the age of 19, but it is not clear what he did for the next thirteen years before going to St Bees Theological College, Cumbria. This was the first college to have been established (in 1816) outside Oxford and Cambridge for the training of priests for the established church. A College Calendar[87n] published in 1858 gave its object as being to "supply a good and economical education for candidates for Holy Orders". Henry evidently qualified successfully from St Bees in 1854, becoming a deacon in 1856 and a priest the following year. He married Louisa Elizabeth Cunnington, a brewer's daughter, in 1859 at King's Cliffe, Northants and two years later was curate of Ayrton, Rutland. He became rector of the small Parish of Draughton, Northants, from 1877 to 1893, and died at Bedford in 1899 aged 79.

Arthur Rousby (born 1822), the other disinherited son, went to sea. He married Elizabeth Abraham, a builder's daughter, in 1857 at Islington but died[88n] only six years later in Shanghai, leaving his widow with three children, the oldest of them five years old, in Peckham. At the time of his death he was master of the steamship "Titian" in the service of the China and Japan Steam Company. Family tradition has it that he died of yellow fever. A picture of him and a photograph of his gravestone in Shanghai have survived (fig. 43, p. 47 and fig. 44).

Figure 44

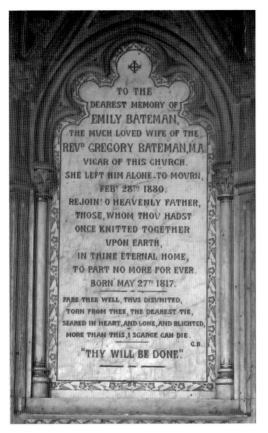

TO THE
DEAREST MEMORY OF
EMILY BATEMAN,
THE MUCH LOVED WIFE OF THE
REVᴰ GREGORY BATEMAN, M.A.
VICAR OF THIS CHURCH.
SHE LEFT HIM ALONE TO MOURN,
FEBᵞ 28ᵀᴴ 1880.
REJOIN! O HEAVENLY FATHER,
THOSE, WHOM THOU HADST
ONCE KNITTED TOGETHER
UPON EARTH,
IN THINE ETERNAL HOME,
TO PART NO MORE FOR EVER.
BORN MAY 27ᵀᴴ 1817.
FARE THEE WELL, THUS DISUNITED,
TORN FROM THEE, THE DEAREST TIE,
SEARED IN HEART, AND LONE, AND BLIGHTED,
MORE THAN THIS, I SCARCE CAN DIE.
G.B.
"THY WILL BE DONE".

Figure 45

Emily Rousby (born 1817), the disinherited daughter, married Rev Gregory Bateman[89n] at Cottisford in 1850. He was a widower and ten years her senior. The year after their marriage they had two servants living in at the Rectory in Tansor, Northamptonshire. Similarly in 1871 they had two servants living in, but by then were at Cold Ashby, in Northants, where he was curate. He later became vicar of that place.

They appear to have had no children. When Emily died in 1880 (fig. 45) Gregory embarked on a major programme of commemorative works. Apart from a conventional headstone in the new cemetery recording his loss, he installed a large tablet in her memory in the church[90] and a stained glass window showing her playing the organ (fig. 46, p. 54), plus a fourth bell in the church tower. A magnificent lych gate was also built at the entrance to the churchyard in her memory costing £400 and incorporating 70 tons of stone.

Charles James Rousby (born 1823) married Emma Harriet La Hai Gill, the daughter of a "Gentleman", at Kensington in 1850. He also was then described as a "Gentleman". They had at least one daughter and for many years lived at Stockland in Devon. He described himself at three Censuses as an "Annuitant" and usually had one or two servants living in. But eventually he and his wife ran a residential school in Basingstoke, their household in 1871 including two Governesses (Musical and French), nine girl pupils aged from 9 to 17, one Under Teacher, a housemaid and a cook. They eventually retired to Maidstone where she died in 1901 and Charles James died in 1905.

The youngest of this generation, Lucy (born 1827), married Edward Henry Wynne at Cottisford in 1858 when she was 31 years old. He was a widower, variously described[91n] as a gentleman and a bank manager. Lucy appears to have had no offspring. Edward Wynne was dead by 1871 and she never remarried, living on the coast first at Worthing and then at Maidstone where she died in 1906 aged 79. Her residence in Maidstone had been only ½ mile (0.8 km) from where her brother Charles James had been living in 1905 and they may well have kept in touch in their old age.

Looking back over what we have been able to learn about the fortunes of this generation of the Rousby family, it does seem that the two sons who were disinherited by their father did not fare as well in life as their more favoured siblings: their wives certainly did not come from well-connected families. Emily was the exception: although she had been disinherited, the man she married – Rev Gregory Bateman – evidently had considerable private means.

The eldest son, Edwards Rousby, continued to live at Cottisford House for some years after his father's death, at least until 1851 when he and his two unmarried sisters were recorded there at the time of the Census. But he then relinquished the lease to Serjeant Parry, a County Court

Judge[92]. In May 1854, at the age of 35, he married Louisa Catherine Johns (daughter of a Brevet Major, Royal Marines) at Dalwood , Devon and the following year was living in Northamptonshire at Irthlingborough, where their first child was born in February 1855. Considerable correspondence[93] between Edwards Rousby and Messrs Brown and Merry, Agents of Eton College, during 1855 survives and shows that he was then keen to return to Cottisford House – if the terms were right – and he did so in August of that year.

The next generation of Rousbys proved to be less numerous than the previous one. After the daughter born at Irthlingborough their other two children, a son and a daughter, were born and baptised at Cottisford in 1857 and 1858 respectively.

Edwards Rousby died at the age of 56 as the result of an accidental fall in Cottisford House. A report of the inquest on 27th October 1875 at Deddington before C Duffell Faulkner Esq appeared in Jacksons Oxford Journal on 30th October (fig. 47). He was buried under the chancel of the church, a note in the Parish Register recording that the "vault is now full up". He was commemorated in unusually lavish fashion, his name being added to that of his father on the large slab in the centre of the chancel floor, another plaque on the north wall and, eventually, by the provision of stained glass in the large east window, paid for by his widow and two daughters.

His son, E R K Rousby had been educated at Winchester and then at Magdalen College Oxford. He was admitted to the Middle Temple[94] in November 1876, just over a year after his father's death and when he was 20 years of age. He was never called to the Bar and therefore could not have practiced as a Barrister.

The elder of Edwards Rousby's daughters, Edith Lousia Catherine Rousby, married Rudolph Fane de Salis[95n] at Cottisford in 1878 when

Children of Edwards Rousby and his wife Louisa Catherine

Edith Louisa Catherine	born 1855 died 1920
Edwards Richard Kendall	bapt 1857 died 1928
Josephine Emily Frances	bapt 1858 died 1952

On the 27th instant, at Cottesford, on the body of E. Rousby, Esq. The sudden death of this benevolent and highly-respected gentleman has cast a gloom over the parish of Cottesford and the neighbourhood. He was well known in the circles of the nobility and gentry, having been born at Souldern House in 1819. The Rev. C. S. Harrison was Foreman of the Jury. Mr. J. H. Gough, barrister, was also present at the enquiry. After the usual formalities had been gone through, the Coroner proceeded to take the evidence of Jas. Baines, butler to the deceased, and of Mr. Walter Moore, surgeon, Brackley. It appeared that about half-past seven o'clock on Sunday evening last the butler, as he was sitting in the kitchen, heard a fall on a back staircase leading to a lumber room. Feeling alarmed, he started at once to see what it was, when he heard his master call out to him. Baines found Mr. Rousby on the top of the first landing, at the bottom of a second flight of stairs leading to the lumber room, and asked him if he felt giddy. He replied, "No; I caught my foot against a little box." Deceased then pointed it out, as it stood on the top step close to the door of the lumber room. The deceased then asked his butler to put the box into the lumber room, and then lock the door and give him the key. He would not let Mrs. Rousby be called, as he said he thought he should soon be better. In a few minutes he said he felt faint, and asked the butler for some spirits. Some brandy and water was given to him by Mrs. Rousby. After that he was carried down to the drawing-room. With assistance the deceased managed to walk a little, and about ten o'clock he was got to bed, where he became much worse. Mr. Moore was sent for, and he arrived about eleven o'clock the same night, and then Mr. Hoctor later on. Mr. F. Symonds, of Oxford, also saw the deceased about nine o'clock on Monday morning, when the medical men had a consultation, and were of opinion that a blood vessel on the brain of the deceased had been ruptured by a blow, and that the case was a perfectly hopeless one. The deceased related to Mr. Moore when he first arrived the circumstances of the fall, and said that he had struck his right temple and that his head ached fearfully. The deceased did not remain conscious any length of time after making these remarks to Mr. Moore, but gradually became worse, and expired about ten o'clock the same night. The Jury returned a verdict in accordance with the evidence, and remitted their fees to the poor box.

Figure 47

she was 23. Rudolph had been educated at Eton and was the second son of Henry de Salis, the wealthy Rector of the nearby village of Fringford. Rudolph described himself at the time of his marriage to Edith Rousby as a "Gentleman". For a while he was a Civil Engineer, but resigned the profession after about ten years and in 1891 described himself as "Living on own means". He and Edith seem to have lived in Acton for most of their married life, but at the time of the 1891 Census they were staying with his parents in Epsom, together with his younger brother (a barrister). His father's household at that time included 15 resident servants comprising butler, two footmen, groom, cook and ten maids of seven different varieties. The couple appear to have had no children and when Edith died in 1920 her husband was the only beneficiary under her Will.

The younger of the two daughters, Josephine Emily Frances Rousby, married Edward Thomas Worley at Cottisford in 1884 when she was 26. He was a solicitor from Stony Stratford, three years older than she was. Her brother and sister were both witnesses. The couple had two daughters and were living at Calverton in both 1891 and 1901, with two servants living in. He was clerk to the magistrates and burial board in Buckingham[96], where he had his office. By the time Josephine made her Will in 1943 she was a widow and living at Stratford House, Stony Stratford. For a brief personal memory of her in her later years and a photograph, see Appendix B.

Edwards Rousby had made his Will the year before he died, when all three of his children were still minors. He directed that his widow, Louisa Catherine, should have the use and enjoyment of household furniture paintings prints books musical instruments plate glass china linen and other household effects. She lived on at Cottisford House for a further 42 years with their son, Edwards Richard Kendall Rousby, until her death in 1917. At the time of the 1881 Census she was listed as head of the household, although her son was by then well over 21 years of age. However, by the time of the next Census, in 1891, their nominal roles had reversed and he was listed as head of the household.

Both of them paid regular visits to Cottisford School during this period. They would have been astounded – and probably indignant – had they known that one of the young pupils, the unassuming daughter of a tradesman living in Juniper Hill, was storing up memories of them and would write them down many years later under the name of the Bracewell family in "Lark Rise" for all the world to read.

The portrait that Flora Thompson painted of Louisa Catherine was not a friendly one[97]. The squire's mother

"still reigned as Lady of the Manor … a tall, haughty, and still handsome old dame … As she got poorer, she got prouder, more overbearing in manner and more acid in tone, and the girls trembled when she came into school …".

And more generally

"It would be almost impossible for anyone born in this century to imagine the pride and importance of such small country gentlepeople in the 'eighties. As far as was known, the Bracewells (ie the Rousby's) were connected with no noble family; they had but little land, kept up but a small establishment, and were said in the village and hamlet to be 'poor as crows'. Yet, by virtue of having been born into a particular caste and living in the 'big house' of the parish, they expected to reign over their poorer neighbours and to be treated by them with the deference due to royalty".

Flora Thompson's memories of E R K Rousby were less hostile

*"Squire at the Manor House, known as 'our Squire', not out of any particular affection
or respect, but in contradistinction to the richer and more important squire in a neighbouring parish, was at that time unmarried, though verging on middle age ... Squire himself
called at the school once a year; but nobody felt nervous when his red, jovial face appeared
in the doorway ... He took his responsibilities less seriously[98n] than his mother did hers;
spending most of his days roaming the fields and spinneys with a gun under his arm and a
brace of spaniels at his heels"*

In considering these comments it is as well to bear in mind that Flora Thompson's father was, by her own account[99], "a Liberal of pronounced views". So her comments about the
squire's mother and the place of such "gentry" in the community are perhaps not unexpected.
She rather exaggerated the decline in the numbers of staff employed at Cottisford House when
she wrote that

*"By the middle of the 'eighties a cook and a house-parlourmaid sat down at meals
in the vast servants' hall where a large staff had formerly feasted".*

In fact, staff numbers had soon declined from six in 1841 to four from 1851 to 1881 and then
to three in all the Censuses up to and including 1911. But Flora was correct when she wrote of
the family becoming poorer. It is known that E R K Rousby had obtained a £3,000 mortgage[100n]
on the property prior to 1896 and records of "death duty" paid on the estate show that there
had, indeed, been a marked fall in the family's fortunes. When Edwards Rousby died in 1875
his estate was valued at "under £45,000". When his widow died in 1917 her effects were valued
at £1,822-4s-6d and when E R K Rousby died in 1928 his effects were valued at £13,806 – a very
substantial effective reduction, bearing in mind inflation over that period.

Long after Flora Thompson had left the Parish, the
bachelor squire of whom she wrote did, in fact, marry.
In November 1896, at the age of 39, E R K Rousby married 25-year-old Agnes Lilian Whall at Croughton, she
being the step-daughter of the rector there. Presumably
the bride moved into Cottisford House with her husband (and her mother-in-law!) but the marriage did not
last long. Thirteen months later, just before Christmas
1897, they evidently separated and he entered into an
agreement to pay her £100 per annum for life. By the
time of the Census in 1901 she was working as a teacher
in an elementary school in Oxford. She was then living at 85, James Street, Oxford, shown here on a recent
photograph (fig. 48), with a resident servant, while E R
K Rousby and his mother continued to live at Cottisford
House.

When Louisa Catherine Rousby died in 1917 she was
buried in the north-western corner of the churchyard.
E R K Rousby died, childless[101n], in 1928 and was buried
alongside his mother. He was the last of the Cottisford
Rousbys.

Figure 48

12. FROM YORKSHIRE TO COTTISFORD VIA BERMONDSEY

Early in the 20th Century a book[102n] entitled "Oxfordshire Leaders, Social and Political" was published in which a page was devoted to E R K Rousby, then the owner of Cottisford House. In this the following statement appeared:

> *"Mr Rousby's family originally came from Yorkshire, where they were Lords of the Manor of Croome Hall, in the East Riding, for about two hundred years, the last member of the ancient and honourable family who owned it being Henry Edwards Rousby, the great uncle of the present proprietor of Cottisford House".*

This information was no doubt provided by E R K Rousby himself and raises the question – what was it that caused the Rousbys to give up ownership of their substantial Croome estate and move to Oxfordshire?

Surviving records now held at York, Beverley and Hull University confirm that the Rousby family had, indeed, acquired the township of Croome early in the 17th Century. The purchase appears to have been started[103] by one Christopher Rousby in 1618 and later generations of the family increased their holding until it comprised about 1,400 acres (570 hectares, upwards of two square miles).

As was customary, the estate passed in successive generations from father to eldest son but in 1767 the then owner, Henry Rousby, died without issue. In his Will of 1762 he had made complex provisions leaving the Croome estate successively to various male relatives with the intention of ensuring that it would remain in the ownership of the Rousby family. But fate decreed that early deaths and lack of sons would bedevil the family for years.

Initially the Croome estate was to go to Henry Rousby's brother Robert and then, on his death, to any eldest son that he might have. Although married, Robert was already more than 70 years of age when Henry made his Will, and when he died in 1773 evidently left no issue. So the estate then passed, under the terms of Henry's Will to their great nephew Rev Robert James Clay, a grandson of their late sister Ann, on condition that he took the surname Rousby.

R J Clay had been born at Newark in 1732, but on the death of his great uncle Robert he adopted the surname Rousby and moved into Croome House, (fig. 49: pictured in 2007), and remained there until his death in 1793. He was the last Rousby to occupy the property and was buried at the nearby Parish Church at Sledmere. During his lifetime the old church had been largely demolished and replaced at great expense by the wealthy Sykes family living nearby. On the wall of the nave is a later memorial (fig. 50) commemorating these three owners of the Croome estate[104n].

Under Henry Rousby's Will, any son of R J C Rousby would have inherited the property, but there were none[105]. The property should then have passed to John Edwards, grandson of Henry's late sister, Elizabeth. But John Edwards, who lived in Westbury, Wiltshire, had died a bachelor[106] a few months earlier, so the estate passed to his brother Thomas Edwards. Thomas Edwards presumably adopted the surname Rousby, but did not enjoy the ownership of Croome for long. He died intestate in 1796 and the property then evidently passed to his 9-year-old elder son, Henry Edwards Rousby. In the short space of 29 years the estate had been owned by five different people spanning four generations.

Figure 49

Figure 50

Figure 51

Henry Edwards Rousby was the last member of the family to own the Croome estate, as correctly stated in Gaskell's book quoted at the start of this chapter. But to describe him as the great uncle of E R K Rousby may give the impression that their lives overlapped. They did not: Henry Edwards Rousby had been dead 48 years when E R K Rousby was born. He had died a bachelor in June 1809 at the relatively young age of 22.

Three months before his death, Henry Edwards Rousby made a very detailed Will comprising no fewer than 14 pages. Apart from its length, it was unusual in two other respects. First, he left £150 to one of his grandmothers. Secondly he directed that the Croome estate, which had then been in the family's ownership for almost 200 years, was to be sold. Although he thus severed the family's long-standing connections with the area, he did donate £100 to the poor of the hamlet of Croome. A plaque in Sledmere church records this gift (fig. 51), though by the time his affairs were finalised in 1812 the beneficiaries had been widened to cover the poor of the whole Parish of Sledmere.

He had three sisters, all of whom were married by the time he made his Will in March 1809, and he left substantial bequests to them of £6,000, £5,000 and £3,000 in trust for their children. Other generous legacies, including £3,000 to one of his executors, absorbed about another £6,000. When the Croome Estate was sold, as Henry had directed, in 1812 it made just over £60,000. After debts and mortgages had been cleared this left around £37,000 for the sole surviving brother, James Edwards Rousby, who many years later was to become the first member of the Rousby family to live at Cottisford House.

Henry Edwards Rousby's decision to direct the sale of Croome was particularly unusual when he had a younger brother (then aged 17) who could have succeeded to the estate. Two possible reasons for this can be suggested. The first was that he was not a native of Yorkshire nor – originally – a Rousby. He had been born plain Henry Edwards in Bermondsey in 1787. At some stage he, and at least one of his sisters[107n] had moved to Yorkshire, living in the town of Driffield, only six miles (10 km) from Croome. From his Will it is clear that he had a wide range of leisure pursuits – including shooting, fishing and playing the piano – and with friends around London he may not have felt any particularly strong attachment to the property at Croome. It had come into his hands only because his great grandmother, Elizabeth Edwards of Westbury, who had died many years before he was born, had been a Rousby before marriage.

The second possible reason for his decision to direct that the Croome estate be sold relates to the surrounding countryside. Croome was a hamlet within the Parish of Sledmere and the whole estate lay within that Parish. Croome House was not particularly large or distinguished, in marked contrast to the property known as Sledmere House which lay less than a mile (1.6 km) away to the south. This latter was the home of the Sykes family, very successful merchants since the 17th Century, and by 1809 owners of more than 30,000 acres (12,100 hectares, upwards of 45 square miles) of the surrounding Yorkshire Wolds.

The recent Victoria County History volume describing this portion of the county states[108] that in the early 17th Century William Rousby of Croome was one of only seven individuals in the district having, or claiming, the status of "gentleman". By the late 17th Century there were only three families of resident gentry, one of which was the Rousbys: and by the mid 18th Century only the Rousbys remained.

But then, in 1748, Richard Sykes moved to Sledmere where, in the words of the VCH, "he and his successors created one of the great estates of eastern England". It was not long before disputes arose between the two families. In the 1750's "angry letters" passed[109] between Richard Sykes and Henry Rousby concerning the former's right to enclose a large mere in front of Sledmere House. And in 1776 Rev James Rousby petitioned[110] against a Bill seeking to enclose the Parish which had been promoted by Christopher Sykes. By 1809 H E Rousby may well have felt that the owners of Croome House would be for ever over-shadowed by the conspicuously successful Sykes family who owned much of the immediately surrounding land. Sledmere House was then, and continues to be today, an exceptionally fine country house and its proximity must surely have been a factor behind Henry Edwards Rousby's decision to abandon Croome.

Whatever the reason for H E Rousby's decision, which was clearly taken with great deliberation, he seems to have been an imprudent young man. Because his brother was a minor, the Court of Chancery was much involved with the sale of the estate and with the general administration of H E Rousby's Will. Copies of many of the Court's relevant records have survived, being held today amongst the Sykes papers by the University of Hull. Amongst them is a note[111] showing that the Executors, in seeking to ensure that all his debts had been paid, came across a memorandum signed by H E Rousby and Sir Clement Briggs dated the sixteenth day of April 1808 whereby it "appeared that Sir Clem^t^ Briggs betted with the said Testator one hundred guineas on the event of a Battle between two Prize Fighters …" (fig. 52).

Only a month before making this wager H E Rousby had attained the age of 21. Staking a hundred guineas – a considerable sum at that time – on the result of a prize fight suggests a distinctly spendthrift side to his character. During the last year of his life he obtained two mortgages[112] on the Croome estate for £2,000 and £3,000 respectively and had he lived much longer it seems likely that his brother James might not have received the comfortable inheritance which led him eventually to Cottisford.

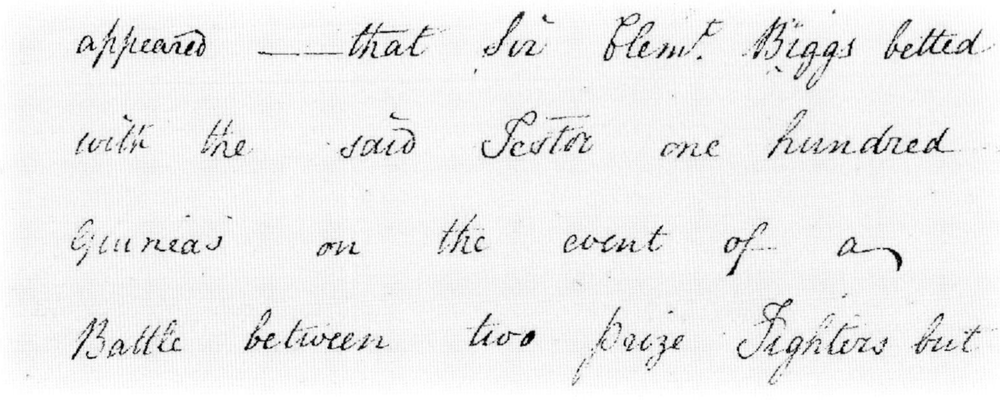
appeared — that Sir Clem^t^ Briggs betted
with the said Testor one hundred
Guineas on the event of a
Battle between two Prize Fighters but

Figure 52

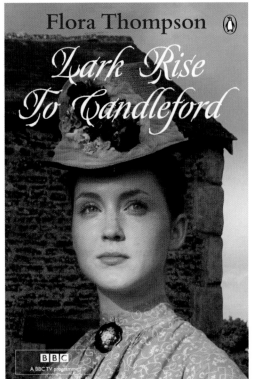

ABOVE: Figure 43 (page 38) Captain Arthur Rousby.

LEFT: Figure 81 (page 81) Reprint of Flora Thompson's trilogy produced by Penguin in 2008 by arrangement with the BBC.

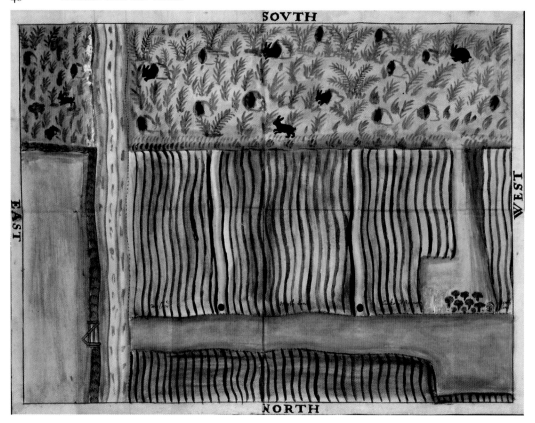

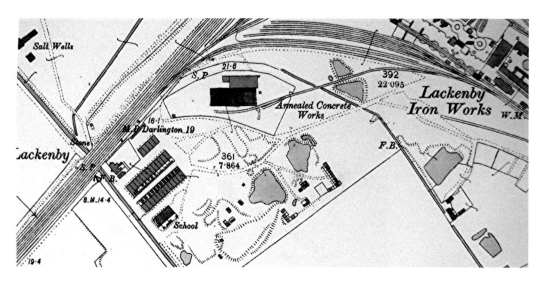

TOP: *Figure 88 An unusual plan in Eton College archives showing part of Cottisford Parish known as Cuckolds Burrows (or Borough). A field with this name (coloured brown) can be seen on the southern boundary of the Parish adjoining Hardwick Heath on Fig 37, page 52. The strip of green across the bottom of the plan is twice labelled "Heath Lane" but this is difficult to reconcile with the detailed map on Fig 37. The plan is 17 1/2" x 13 1/2" (445 x 340 mm) and possibly of the early 17th century.*

ABOVE: *Figure 60 (page 65) The area of the iron works at Low Lackenby as shown on the first edition 1/2500 OS map of Yorkshire 7. The estate of 31 small terrace houses is coloured pink on the left and two of the circular blast furnaces can be seen top right.*

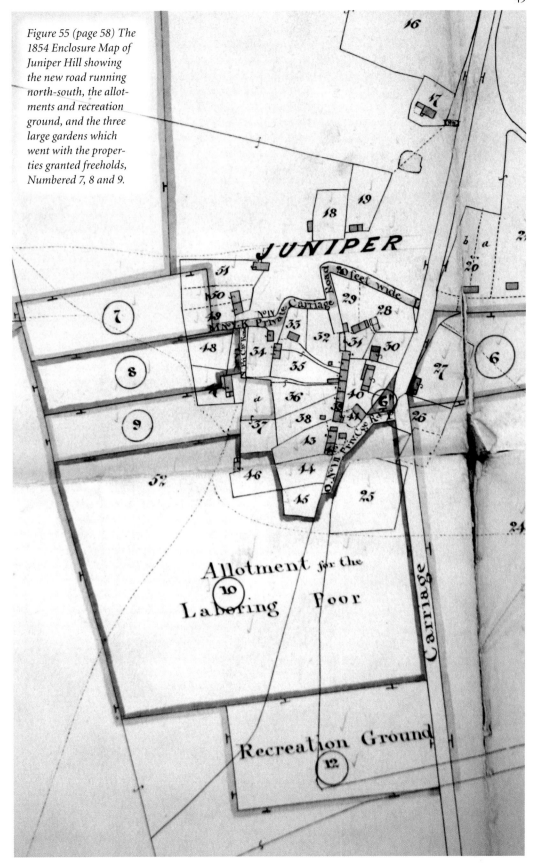

Figure 55 (page 58) The 1854 Enclosure Map of Juniper Hill showing the new road running north-south, the allotments and recreation ground, and the three large gardens which went with the properties granted freeholds, Numbered 7, 8 and 9.

Figure 37 (pages 29 & 55) The upper part of a map of the Parish to the scale of 3 chains to an inch (i.e. 1 to 2376) in Eton College Archives. The map is about 2′ 9″ x 3′ 2″ (850 x 965 mm) and is believed to date from the late 18th Century. It shows the uncultivated area known as "The Heath" which formed the western part of the Parish, with various tracks criss-crossing it, and many of the Medieval strips still remaining on the arable parts at that time. At some later date the road through Juniper Hill, constructed during the enclosure of 1854, was added to the map in pencil. The lower half of this map is on the following spread. There is no north point on the map: we have inserted one for clarity.

Figure 38 (pages 29 & 55) The lower part of the Parish map from the previous spread.

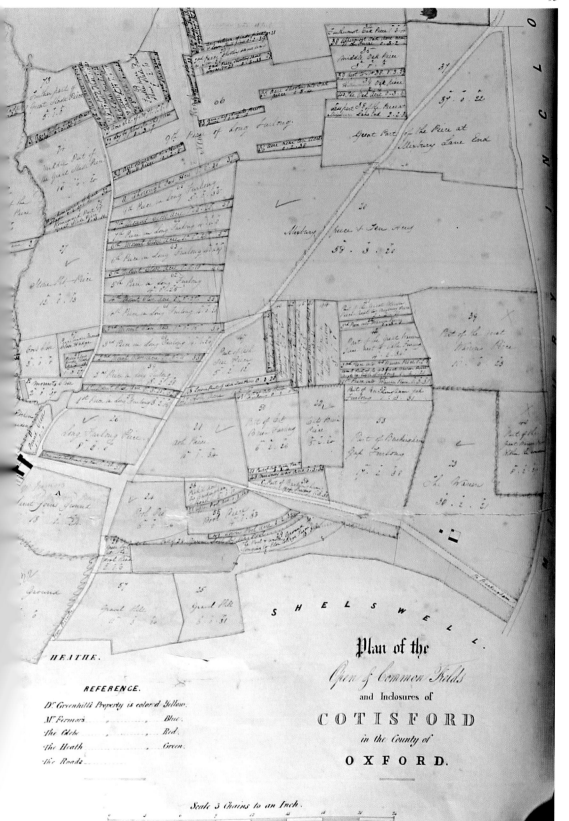

Plan of the
Open & Common Fields
and Inclosures of
COTISFORD
in the County of
OXFORD.

HEATHE.

REFERENCE.

Dr Greenhill's Property is color'd Yellow.
Mr Fermor's ,, ,, Blue.
The Glebe ,, ,, Red.
The Heath ,, ,, Green.
The Roads

Scale 3 Chains to an Inch.

BELOW: *Figure 1 (page 3) The surviving tower at the Abbey of Bec in Normandy.* RIGHT: *Figure 46 (page 39) The commemorative window in Cold Ashby church showing Emily Bateman (formerly Rousby) playing the organ.* BOTTOM: *Figure 78 (page 80) The memorial to Second World War dead, including Flora Thompson's son Peter, in Royal Avenue Gardens, Dartmouth.*

13. ENCLOSURE!

For many of us today the word "Enclosure" conjures up little more than memories of history lessons and examination questions. We may dimly remember something of the collaborative farming long ago of innumerable "strips" in open fields, and a procedure under which (with the encouragement of Government) the strips disappeared and land tenure was dramatically reorganised – against the wishes of many people and to the substantial benefit of a few. But it all seems rather distant today.

For Flora Thompson the word had much more immediate significance. She referred to the Enclosure Acts on the first page of "Lark Rise" and, because the final enclosure of Cottisford took place relatively late – in 1854 – there were old folk still living in Juniper Hill when she was a child who recounted to her[113] their bitter memories of its effects, resulting in the loss of both income and independence. In particular, Old Sally "could just remember the Rise when it stood in a wide expanse of open heath, with juniper bushes and furze thickets and close, springy, rabbit-bitten turf". And Sally's father had been able to keep "… a cow, geese, poultry, pigs, and a donkey-cart to carry his produce to the market town. He could do this because he had commoners' rights and could turn his animals out to graze, and cut furze for firing …".

In Blomfield's account[114] of the nearby Parish of Lower Heyford he included a remarkable map of that Parish in 1606 showing more than 400 strips of the old Open Field system, most of them about an acre (0.4 hectare) in extent, but some less than half that size. Even today, some parts of Oxfordshire which have not been put to the plough for centuries still show the characteristic slightly S-shaped pattern of ridge and furrow which developed as a result of repeated ploughing of the strips with teams of oxen. There are particularly clear-cut areas on either side of the Chiltern railway line south-east of Bicester and on the undulating ground east of the M40 at Banbury.

There is no vestige remaining today of the old pattern of ridge and furrow which must at one time have covered most of Cottisford Parish other than the Heath. There is however, one historic document which shows clearly the remnants of the open fields through the survival in separate ownership of many of the original Medieval strips. This document[115], in the ownership of Eton College, is a map of the Parish dating from the late 18th Century. This shows that by then many of the Medieval strips in the areas suitable for arable farming had already been combined with their neighbours or had disappeared altogether in a process of piecemeal, gradual enclosure. This map is reproduced in two sections as figures 37 and 38 on pages 50–53.

By the middle of the Nineteenth Century only the Heath forming the western part of the Parish remained un-enclosed. There had been attempts[116] to enclose it in 1761, 1777 and 1809, but they had all failed after strong local opposition. But the passing of a comprehensive Parliamentary Act[117] in 1848, covering about twenty Parishes in various counties, including Cottisford, allowed the process finally to be set in motion here. The part of Eton College's map showing the heath is shown on pages 50 and 51.

Once again this threat of enclosure led, inevitably, to strong opposition. The residents of Juniper Hill had two main reasons for concern at the changes proposed. First, they would lose their rights to grazing on the heath and cutting useful furze there. Secondly, and even more importantly, their cottages had been built on common land to which they had no title. So, although some of the cottages had been there for almost 100 years, those who occupied them were technically "encroachers" or "squatters".

The first formal notice of the proposed "Inclosure of arable, pasture and waste lands" in Cottisford Parish appeared in Jackson's Oxford Journal in January 1848 together with the announcement of a meeting to be held at the Crown Inn, Brackley on the 25th of that month "for the purpose of hearing any objections which may be made to the proposed Inclosure".

The process of submitting and receiving objections evidently proceeded slowly over the next three years and early in February 1851 Wm Brown of Tring wrote[118] to Eton College regretting that "… the matter should have been held back so long as it in some degree makes the difficulty greater in dealing with the squatters …". At the same time another of the College's correspondents wrote[119] that "… the Estate has suffered great injury by the delay in consequence of the extensive/ and increasing encroachments of the Squatters defying alike the Law and the Landlord …".

But, although the full power of the state and the law was clearly aligned against the residents of Juniper Hill, they were not friendless. Amongst the archives of Eton College is an important letter[120] dated 12th May 1851 written to the College by Rev Dewar, who was at that time Curate of Cottisford. He started his letter by writing that "There is great tribulation at Juniper about the enclosure of the heath and I have been requested by the poor people to write to you on the subject". He soon found that he needed to write more than both sides of the single piece of paper could accommodate, so he superimposed a second set of writing at right angles to the first, as shown in the excerpt (fig. 53). Despite this unusual format, the letter was a powerful one, making a plea which – coming from a man of the cloth – must have been difficult for the authorities to ignore. Having turned the paper, Rev Dewar went on, "It is impossible to tell what will become of the wretched poor at Cottisford if their houses are pulled down and they are turned adrift".

He also pointed out that the settlement at Juniper had been initiated by the Squire, the Rector and five other landowners in

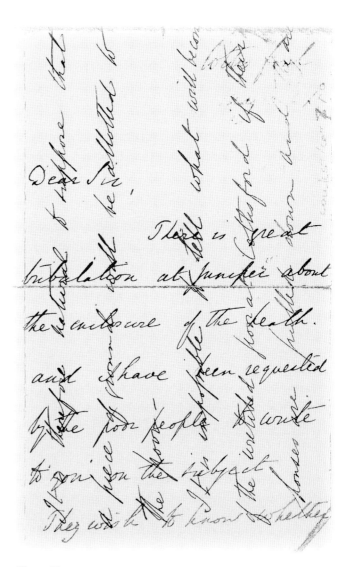

Figure 53

1754 when they arranged (and paid for) the building of the first two houses there. In other words the start had been a charitable act by the better-off residents of the Parish, not an "encroachment" by squatters.

Rev Dewar also asked two key questions. First, whether "their houses will be pulled down and their ground ploughed up or that they will be allowed to occupy them on the payment of a fixed rent". And, secondly he asked whether "any plot of ground on the heath will be reserved for the use of the poor".

In that same month[121n] a valuer appointed by the Inclosure Commissioners held what was intended to be the last meeting in Brackley for the receipt of claims in writing. In the following month the valuer deposited a statement of all claims received at "the Farm House occupied by Mr Wood" in Cottisford and allowed a month for the receipt of any objections to the claims.

A week later the Commissioners announced that a meeting was to be held in Brackley to "enquire into the circumstances under which encroachments have been made from the said lands". The vital issue of ownership of the cottages at Juniper Hill and their gardens was now right at the top of the agenda. In August 1851 the valuer held a further meeting at Brackley to examine and determine claims. This must have produced a considerable volume of submissions and it was seven months before the valuer deposited copies of all further claims at "the Farm House in the occupation of Mr Wood": any objections were to be submitted by 15th March 1852. In the meantime, the Commissioners' firm intention to proceed with enclosure was demonstrated by an invitation to Roadmakers to submit tenders in March for making the necessary roads, and by the announcement in April that various public roads, bridleways and footpaths were to be diverted or discontinued.

It was also in March 1852 that the strong feelings of Parishioners boiled over and led to William Bachelor of Juniper Hill being charged by William Wood (of the Farm House, one of the likely beneficiaries of enclosure) with assaulting him. The case was eventually "amicably arranged".

In July 1852 the valuer deposited a schedule of all claims and objections at "Mr Wood's Farm House" together with his determinations thereon for the inspection of all interested persons.

These "determinations" created so much dissatisfaction that 40 Parishioners, largely but not entirely living in Juniper Hill, engaged an attorney who then gave formal notice of their desire to have their claims reheard and determined by a Commissioner or an Assistant Commissioner. This procedure evidently took place and in January 1853 the Commissioners deposited copies of their determinations at the house of Mr Richard Wood for inspection.

The dissatisfaction of residents was not abated and when one W H Richards went to Juniper Hill to serve notices a few months later he was assaulted by William Bachelor and George Price. George Price was fined 5s with 9s 6d costs: William Bachelor was fined more, 10s 6d plus 9s 6d costs, because of having previously been charged with a similar offence, and each was to be imprisoned in default of payment.

Matters came to a head in July 1853 when a list (fig. 54) was published of 42 residents who had been charged with refusing to give up possession of lands at Juniper Hill after being given two months' notice. Warrants were issued by the magistrates for them to be ejected.

This list shows that the whole community was holding out against the authorities. Virtually every "Head of household" from the enumerators' returns at the Census of Juniper Hill two years earlier was on the list, together with sixteen further individuals. In some cases these were sons clearly determined to support their families: in others they were men living elsewhere in the Parish who presumably had still enjoyed rights to grazing and furze on the Heath.

Three weeks later the authorities took decisive action. A party of 20 men descended on the hamlet, including constables armed with pick axes which could be used for demolishing buildings. The confrontation appears to have lasted for two days, at the end of which a compromise was reached. Three of the cottagers, John Moss, Robert Moss and John Price, were granted the freeholds of their homes together with substantial gardens (numbered 7, 8 and 9 on the map[122] – fig. 55, p. 49). One other person, John Painter, was granted the freehold of a small detached parcel of land well to the north of the hamlet, abutting the Northamptonshire border, which he had presumably already brought under cultivation. The remainder of the cottagers were granted leases on their dwellings for 14 years at 5s 0d per year (about 1% of a labourer's income) and retained the crops from their gardens, in return for which they formally gave up possession.

By sticking together and holding out resolutely for so long the residents of Juniper Hill had obtained significant concessions. And the intervention of Rev D E Dewar[123n] may have been very helpful. The church had considerable influence in those mid-Victorian times and his concern about what would happen if the houses were pulled down and the wretched poor "turned adrift" is unlikely to have fallen on deaf ears. His suggestion of a fixed rent was adopted (at a nominal figure) and when the Enclosure Award was finally published in 1854 it provided eight acres of allotments immediately adjacent to the hamlet – an average of about ¼ acre for each household, which no doubt proved invaluable in the tough years that lay ahead. Flora Thompson recorded[124] how, thirty years later, "The men took great pride in their gardens and allotments … They ate plenty of green food, all home-grown and freshly pulled".

Even though the long dispute about the enclosure had, at long last, been settled, there was still one final court appearance to take place (fig. 56). In its issue of 3rd September 1853 the Oxford Chronicle reported that Joseph Collett had been charged with being "guilty of misconduct in his duty as constable". Joseph lived at the Warren in Cottisford (being recorded there in both 1851 and 1861) and at one time had been a farm bailiff. Having been appointed as one of the two Parish Constables he evidently took a keen interest in the authorities' actions against so many residents of the Parish and his name was included in the published list of 42 objectors (fig. 54). It was recorded that he "felt annoyed at the Juniper Hill ejectment proceedings" and that when officers came to Juniper Hill to carry them into effect he "used irritable expressions of disapprobation". It was judged that this might have led to a breach of the peace and cost him a £2 8s fine plus 12s costs. That was a considerable sum of money and, although there is no record of the phrases he used in his "irritable expressions of disapprobation", one can only hope that he felt better for having said them!

After more than 150 years the enclosure is now a very distant memory and its residual effects on today's residents are wholly beneficial. The eight acres of allotments and the two acres of recreation ground are considerable assets for the Parish. Both are now included in the Juniper Hill Conservation Area, which emphasises their continuing importance to the community.

BICESTER PETTY SESSIONS, JULY 22.

Before H. Peyton, and W. Style, Esqs.

COTTISFORD ENCLOSURE.—William Moss, Henry Tebby, James Tebby, George Price, Henry Price, Joseph Collett, William Collett, Charles Cripps, William Batchelor, Thomas Harris, John Cripps, George Aston, James Ashton, Thos. Ashton, Daniel Cripps, William Cripps, George Fox, Thomas Hall, Richard Harris, Robert Jeacock, John Judd, John Judd, jun., George Moss, Isaac Moss, James Moss, Joseph Moss, William Moss, Richard Moss, Robert Moss, Thomas Moss, John Price, William Price, Geo. King, James King, James Savin, John Savin, 38, Thomas Savin, John Savin, 48, William Savin, David Tuffrey, George Tuffrey, and James Tuffrey, cottagers and occupiers of land at Juniper Hill, Cottesford, were severally charged by Wm. Kerr, of 8, Cannon Row, Westminster, valuer for the enclosure of lands at Cottesford, with refusing to give up possession of certain lands there situated. Mr. Ovenall, solicitor, Leamington, defended. Proof of Mr. Kerr's being the valuer was put in: that claims had been determined by legally-appointed assistant commissioners; that 2 months' notice had been given to the defendants, and that they still held possession. The hearing of the cases occupied some time. Warrants were issued for ejectment. The defendants had resided at Juniper Hill for various periods, and then formed a colony.

Figure 54

A CONSTABLE IN TROUBLE.—Joseph Collett, one of the constables of the parish of Cottisford was, by Superintendent Moulden, charged with having, on the 16th of August, been guilty of misconduct in his duty as constable. It appeared that the accused felt annoyed at the Juniper Hill ejectment proceedings, and that on the officers carrying them into effect he used irritable expressions of disapprobation, and which were considered to be calculated if acted on to lead to a breach of the peace. He was convicted in £2 8s. fine, and 12s. costs.

Figure 56

14. THE FLIGHT FROM THE LAND

Over a period of many centuries most of Cottisford's inhabitants were inescapably tied to working on the land, and for much of that time the number of people living in the Parish probably did not fluctuate a great deal. The rough estimate (in Chapter 2) of 60 to 75 inhabitants at the time of the Domesday Survey in 1086 may be compared with the figure of 105 when the first National Census took place more than 700 years later in 1801. The only major changes during that long period are likely to have resulted from catastrophic events like the Black Death of 1348–49 when some communities, such as the neighbouring Parish of Tusmore[125], were virtually wiped out by disease.

The first half of the 19th Century witnessed a remarkable change when the population suddenly burgeoned in an unprecedented manner. From the figure of 105 in 1801 the number of people living in Cottisford soared to 269 in 1861. This was the time of the great Victorian "Baby Boom", and the number of houses in the Parish also increased sharply (fig. 57). But, despite some increase in the area of land available for agriculture with the enclosure of Cottisford Heath in 1854, the scope for employment on the land was clearly insufficient to cope with such a huge increase, especially as increasing mechanisation was making farming less labour-intensive.

The overwhelming importance of agriculture as virtually the only source of employment in the Parish during this period is illustrated by information to be found in the Baptismal Register. In 1813 the practice commenced of recording the occupation of the father at almost every baptism. During the remainder of the 19th Century a total of 546 baptisms was thus recorded in the Parish, and in 476 (i.e. 87%) of these the father was a farm labourer. Apart from the parson and the squire, and servants in a very small number of households, nearly all the other occupations recorded were associated with the land, such as shepherds, gamekeepers and one or two farmers.

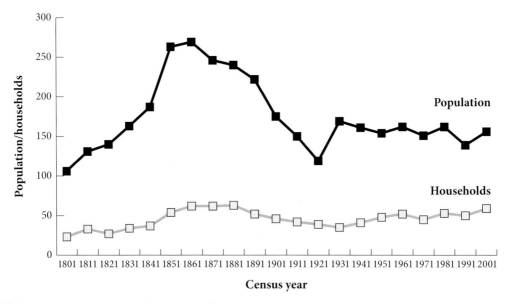

Figure 57

Writing of the last quarter of the century, Flora Thompson recorded[126] that many of the young girls "went into service" in the houses of local gentry, while some of the young men joined the army for "a little mild soldiering". She was particularly familiar with the latter because of her brother Edwin's service with the West Yorkshire Regiment from 1899 to 1907. But those two sources of employment were mainly suitable for youngsters before marriage, less so for those who were older. By 1901 the population of the Parish had declined by a third to 175 and it continued to fall in the early years of the 20th Century. This sharp decline cannot be accounted for by death – throughout the 19th Century there were in each decade roughly twice as many baptisms as burials in the Parish. A considerable exodus from the Parish clearly took place in the later part of the 19th Century and we are fortunate that this can now be traced in some detail.

Mention has been made in earlier chapters of the value to historians of the enumerators' returns from each of the decennial censuses from 1841 to 1901. Their usefulness and availability have been greatly enhanced in recent years by computerised methods and publication of copies on the web. Transcripts are now readily available of all the many millions of enumerators' returns, together with indexes: the associated search engines provide a powerful tool for locating individuals and tracing their movement between one census and the next. In all the censuses from 1851 onwards, the name of the place "where born" was recorded for every individual, so it is now possible to track many individuals who gave their birthplace as Cottisford or Juniper Hill in any of the Censuses.

The example taken from the 1881 Census (fig. 58), illustrates the wealth of information that can be gleaned from such records. William Cripps and his wife had both been born in Cottisford and were now living at Low Lackenby (on Teesside). The birthplaces of three of their children show that since leaving Cottisford they had lived in Northamptonshire at Heyford and later in Yorkshire at (h)Ardsley. For the first time there is now the possibility of tracing the principal movements of everyone in the land, right down to the humblest, whose lives had hitherto been largely hidden in obscurity.

Some emigrants from Cottisford managed to find employment outside the agricultural sector without moving very far. Thus, Thomas Hall, born here in 1848, became a shoemaker in Buckinghamshire, at Loughton, and was recorded there in 1871, 1881 and 1891. William Savin, born here in 1847, moved to the village of Wilby near Wellingborough where he married a local girl and in 1871 was a groom and coachman. By 1881 they had moved with their growing

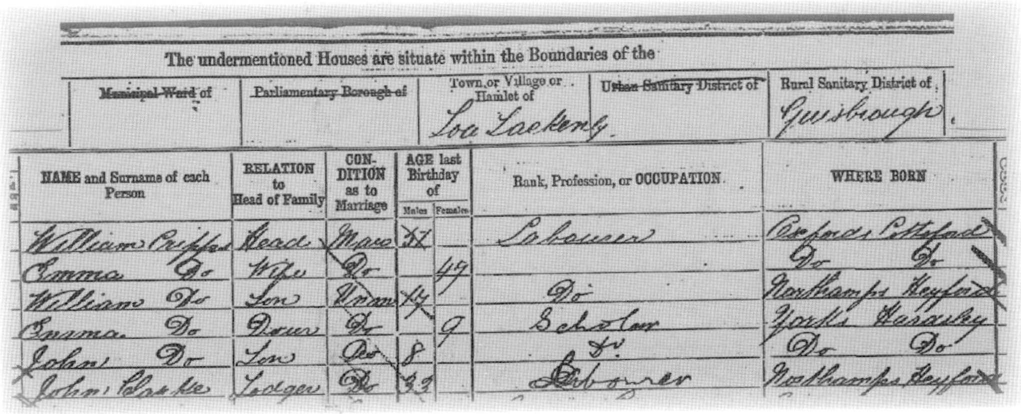

The undermentioned Houses are situate within the Boundaries of the

Municipal Ward of	Parliamentary Borough of	Town or Village or Hamlet of	Urban Sanitary District of	Rural Sanitary District of
		Low Lackenby		Guisbrough

NAME and Surname of each Person	RELATION to Head of Family	CONDITION as to Marriage	AGE last Birthday of Males	AGE last Birthday of Females	Rank, Profession, or OCCUPATION	WHERE BORN
William Cripps	Head	Mar	57		Labourer	Oxford Cottisford
Emma Do	Wife	Do		49		Do Do
William Do	Son	Unm	14		Do	Northamps Heyford
Emma Do	Daur	Do		9	Scholar	Yorks Hardsley
John Do	Son	Do	8		Do	Do Do
John Clarke	Lodger	Do	33		Labourer	Northamps Heyford

Figure 58

family to a cottage in the nearby village of Ecton (notable today as the ancestral home of Benjamin Franklin and a place of pilgrimage for many American visitors). William was still a coachman at that time, but then they moved into the Three Horseshoes Inn in Ecton where he was the publican in 1891 and 1901. (This pub, said to have been built on the site of the village forge worked by Benjamin Franklin's ancestors, continues to this day).

A few others managed to obtain employment elsewhere in occupations not far removed from agriculture, particularly gardening. Thus Henry Baines, born here in 1850, moved to Penshurst in Kent and took up gardening. In 1871 he was single, living as a lodger in the Gardener's House, but later he married a local girl and appears to have lived in Kent for the rest of his life, being described as a retired gardener there in 1901.

Many others had to go further afield and take up entirely new occupations in order to obtain jobs. Frederick Moss, born in 1836, started life here as an agricultural labourer but then moved to Cheshire. In 1871, 1881 and 1891 he was living at Monks Copenhall in that county and employed in various trades connected with the railways. He had married a girl from Buckinghamshire (a lace maker) and it appears from the birthplaces of several of their children that they must have lived for a time at Crewe (a major railway centre). Samuel Cripps, born here in 1861, was also employed on the railways in 1891 and 1901, living at Carlton, Notts and married to a local girl. One of his cousins, Thomas Cripps, born here in 1856, was working on the railways at Finedon, Northants in 1881, 1891 and 1901, married to a local girl and raising a large family there.

Inevitably, some of the emigrants were drawn to London. Daniel Paxton, born at Cottisford in 1854 moved to Marylebone with his parents by 1871 and became a bricklayer. He married a girl from Essex and they moved around, no doubt following work, and were recorded in 1881, 1891 and 1901 living at Marylebone, Croydon and Lambeth: the birthplaces recorded for their children indicate that they had also lived in Kent. Another who went from Cottisford to London was John Bachelor. Born here in 1836 he started his working life here as an agricultural labourer, being recorded as such in 1861 (aged 24) when he was living at Kennel Cottages. The following year he married Elizabeth Savin, also from Cottisford, and their first child was born here in 1863. But they did not stay in the Parish. He was recorded in the 1871, 1881 and 1891 Censuses as a carman or general labourer in Kensington: by 1901 they had moved to Wembley, where he was still working as a general labourer.

The pressure on many such emigrants not to rely on a single breadwinner is well illustrated by this family. John Bachelor's wife Elizabeth was shown working as a laundress in three successive Censuses and in 1881 their eldest daughter aged 17 was also a laundress. By 1891 they had three unmarried daughters in employment, the eldest still as a laundress, the next as a dressmaker, and the youngest, aged 15, as an electrical lamp mounter. (Relatives back in Cottisford must surely have marvelled at news of this – electricity did not reach the Parish until sixty years later!)

Several of the families also took in one or more boarders or lodgers. Thus, in the example illustrated on page 61 the Cripps family in Yorkshire had taken in a lodger who had originated from Heyford in Northamptonshire, where they had previously lived.

The jobs taken on by young men from the Parish when they moved elsewhere were very varied. Edward Collett, born here in 1851, was a labourer in an iron store at King's Sutton in 1871, but he then moved to the Birmingham area and was recorded there in 1881, 1891 and 1901 as a saddler and harness maker. He had married a girl from Helmdon and one of their sons also became a harness maker. Two brothers, Henry T Mansfield and James Mansfield, born here in

1848 and 1854 respectively, found employment in the brewing trade at Horninglow near Burton on Trent where they were both recorded as living in 1881 and 1891, and Henry also in 1901. A probable relative of theirs, Frederick G Mansfield who had been born here in 1871, also went to the same village of Horninglow near Burton on Trent, and married a local girl. He was a joiner's labourer there in 1891 and a wood sawyer in 1901. Many of the emigrants seem to have stuck to one trade, more or less, throughout their working lives but another relative, Henry J Mansfield born here in 1862 was recorded at Lea Marston, Warwickshire, in three successive Censuses as a miller's apprentice in 1881; as a domestic groom in 1891; and as a traction engine driver in 1901.

Another Frederick Moss, born here in 1862, became a prison warder, being recorded at Wandsworth in 1891 and at Springfield in Essex in 1901. James Tebby, born at Cottisford in 1848, became a policeman in London, recorded as a Constable at St George's Hanover Square in 1881 and as a Sergeant at Paddington in 1891: by 1901 he had left the police force and was working on his own account as a grocer at Barking in Essex. Others also joined the police, doubtless an expanding force as the country's population grew, especially in urban areas. Isaac Moss, born here in 1846, was a policeman living with his wife and two children in the Police Station at Baddesley Ensor, Warwickshire, in 1871. And in 1881 George Sabin (or Savin), who had been born here in 1849, was a police constable in Doncaster.

Few of the young men leaving Cottisford seem to have gone to the coast. Exceptions were another James Mansfield, born here in 1857, who was a labourer in a shipyard at Newhaven in 1901: and Walter Savin, born here in 1872 who moved with his parents to Kingston on Thames and then, by 1901, had joined the Royal Navy in Hampshire.

Heavy industry absorbed some of the emigrants. William Cripps, who has already been mentioned in the census return example in figure 58, was born at Juniper Hill in 1830 and was still living here with his parents in 1851, employed as an agricultural labourer. The following year he married Emma Tuffery, a 19-year-old lacemaker also from Juniper Hill, and he continued as an agricultural labourer for at least another 10 years. Although resident here for most of this period the couple also appear to have lived at one time in nearby Evenley, possibly moving so that he could secure work. Eventually they moved to Nether or Lower Heyford, Northamptonshire where William was recorded as an agricultural labourer in 1861 but then started working at blast furnaces there which were fed with ironstone from a small quarry in the parish and other quarries in the vicinity.

The personal history of this Cripps family illustrates not only the mobility forced on them by the need to find work, but also the frequent childbearing of the wife and the fragility of young lives during Victorian times when medical resources were minimal and fatal epidemics occurred at intervals. By the start of 1864, after twelve years of marriage, the family of William and Emma Cripps at Lower Heyford comprised six children, ranging in age from a baby of one to a 12-year-old. Then misfortune struck, and in the short space of four weeks, three of their children died of croup and diphtheria – Esau aged nine who had been born at Evenley, Ambrose aged four who had been born at Cottisford and Mary Ann, aged 13 months, who had been born at Lower Heyford.

William Cripps had now finished for good with agricultural employment and had started a long-term association with the iron industry. At some time prior to 1871 the family moved to Little Harrowden, near Kettering, where an iron works with six blast furnaces had been established in 1866. In 1871 William was a furnace keeper there and two of their sons, George aged 18 and Thomas aged 14 were also furnace labourers there. The younger of these two sons,

Thomas, left the iron industry in about 1875 and, as described above, took up work on the railways in Northamptonshire.

But the rest of this family then made a major move of almost 200 miles (320 km) to Teesside. In 1881 they were living at Low Lackenby adjacent to blast furnaces where William and his son George were both working. By 1891 another son, William (junior) who had been born at Lower Heyford in 1865 had joined them working in the blast furnaces and by 1901 yet another son, John, born in 1873 after the family moved to Yorkshire had also become a blast furnace labourer there. By then, William (senior) was 71 years of age and the oldest worker recorded in the group of 31 terrace houses on the site. It appears[127n] that he continued working as a labourer at the blast furnaces right up to the time of his death in 1909 at the age of 78.

We are fortunate to have a photograph (fig. 59) of this Cripps family taken at Teesside in about 1885. The couple who had originally been born and married here, William Cripps (senior) and his wife Emma, are seated next to each other. The men standing behind them are thought to be two of their elder sons, George and William Cripps (junior), while the young lad on the right is almost certainly their youngest son John Cripps. Next to her father is standing Emma Cripps who never married and in 1901 was living with her father, by then a widower. The other two women are presumably the wives of William and George.

This Cripps family demonstrates in its most striking form the sweeping changes created by the flight from the land. William's father had been an agricultural labourer throughout his life as, in all probability, had been his ancestors. Emma Tuffery's father and paternal grandfather had certainly been agricultural labourers. But the parents and four children had made the long move from Cottisford to the thriving industrial complex at Teesside, and the men spent the rest of their working lives in the heat, smoke and noise of blast furnaces. A greater contrast from agricultural work can scarcely be imagined.

Figure 59

Their living quarters were also utterly different from the scattered rural cottages of Cottisford and Juniper Hill. Throughout the period 1881–1901 they were all recorded as living in the small estate of 31 terrace houses which had been built for workers in about 1871 close to the Lackenby Iron Works. The First Edition 1/2500 Ordnance Survey map (fig. 60, p. 48) shows the estate on the left comprising two rows of 13 houses and one of five, and below them the building described in Bulmer's trade directory of 1890 an "iron school-church". Two of the circular blast furnaces can be seen top right.

Despite all these changes the move had evidently been a financial success. At that time the wages[128] paid to labourers in iron works on Teesside ranged from 2s-6d up to 3s-0d per day. Working a 6-day week would thus have brought in 15s-0d to 18s-0d – a very great improvement on the standard wage of 10s-0d per week recorded[129] by Flora Thompson for agricultural labourers in the Cottisford area. The family photograph was presumably taken to mark some special occasion, but the watch chains worn by William Cripps senior and one of the sons, together with the smart attire of the women, shows that their family had certainly avoided the poverty which marred many urban areas at that time.

The movements of men between Censuses, as described above, are relatively easy to follow. Women are more difficult to trace because the great majority of them married and changed their surnames. A few who remained unmarried can be traced, such as Mary Ann Ariss, born here in 1837, who worked as a cook in Oxford in 1891 and then moved to London: in 1901 she ran a lodging house in Westminster where several relatives from this area were accommodated. Harriett Savin, born here in about 1870, was one of the servants of a family in Bexley, Kent in 1891, and a housemaid in Pembrokeshire in 1901. The latter household illustrates the remarkable amount of domestic employment generated in Victorian times by some of the well-to-do families. The head of the household was a local man aged 53, living on his own means, with his wife and brother-in-law. These three had fifteen servants living in, comprising two footmen, a housekeeper, a lady's maid (from Sweden), three house maids, one kitchen maid, one scullery maid, two laundry maids, a dairy maid and three grooms. Next door in the Bothy lived two gardeners who were probably also employed by this household.

Married women who had been born in Cottisford or Juniper Hill had husbands in occupations just as varied as their emigrant brothers. In 1881 these included a bus conductor in Hornsey and a watch maker's repairer in Syresham, Northamptonshire; in 1891 they included a butcher in Willesden, a coal merchant's contractor in Reigate, and a gymnastic instructor in Huddersfield; and in 1901 they included an assurance agent in Cheshire, a sanitary carter in Worcestershire and a compositor printer in Battersea.

We have described these movements out of the Parish in some detail because the significance of this "flight from the land" has not always been fully recognised. Most of those who moved out were from the younger generation and many of them took up occupations utterly different from work on the farm which had been the lot of their fathers, grandfathers and untold generations before. Some of the trades they entered were quite new – products of the industrial revolution – and most will have embarked on them with no experience and precious little training. Some took wives with them, many married girls raised in their new localities. For the great majority the move was irrevocable – they never returned to live in Cottisford.

The separation from their birthplace was even more marked for those who emigrated overseas. We cannot yet trace their movements with anything like the same facility as those of the emigrants who stayed in this country, but there is no doubt that a considerable number did go abroad – Flora Thompson's brothers[130] Edwin to Canada and Frank to Australia being just two well-known examples.

The effect of all this emigration on those remaining in the Parish must have been profound. Sons and daughters departed to places unknown, and in many cases probably never heard of before. Flora Thompson mentions[131] some of the girls who had "married away" returning to spend a summer fortnight with their parents but such visits will have been difficult, if not impossible, for those located far away with growing families because of the time and expense involved. As one example, we know that Flora Thompson[132] did not bring her first child, Winifred, to meet her grandparents in Juniper Hill until she was six years old. In one family, the Colletts, babies were brought to Cottisford for baptism, four by Edward Collett the harness maker from Birmingham during the period 1874 to 1885 and two by his brother Arthur William Collett, a carpenter living in Oxford, in 1880 and 1881. But these were quite exceptional and some grandparents will seldom – if ever – have seen grandchildren living in distant places. Almost the only contact with such families will have been through the Penny Post.

Towards the end of the Nineteeenth Century, as the population of the Parish diminished sharply, the age structure of those remaining changed significantly. At every Census from 1851 to 1901 the age of every inhabitant was recorded. Figure 61 shows how the proportion of youngsters fell and the proportion of those aged 60 or more almost trebled.

Today, many people are accustomed to having families and friends scattered far and wide. But the marvels of modern travel and communications have made these separations much less painful. To many of the late Victorians the change must have been traumatic. This was particularly so for the oldest couples, as the breadwinning man gradually became unable to carry on with the arduous manual work of a farm labourer. With sons and daughters now living far away, the prospects for such elderly couples must have seemed bleak.

Eventually, the introduction of the old age pension in 1909 provided some financial support for those past working, and this was greeted with huge relief and thankfulness. Writing of Juniper Hill in the Chapter on "Survivals" in "Lark Rise" Flora Thompson related[133] how "… there were one or two poorer couples, just holding on to their homes, but in daily fear of the workhouse … When, twenty years later, the Old Age Pensions began, life was transformed for such aged cottagers. They were relieved of anxiety ".

But the traditional close family structure of the rural community, which had provided remarkable stability and contentment, had been largely swept away for ever by the flight from the land.

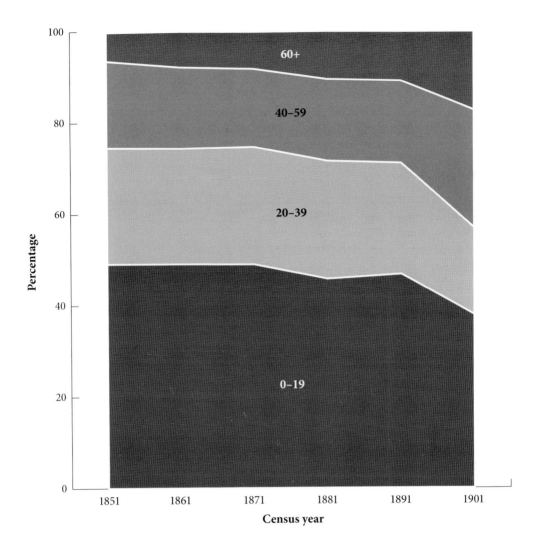

Figure 61

15. THE PARISH'S WAR DEAD

One of our principal aims when we started researching the history of Cottisford Parish in 1995 was to find and place on record details of the twelve young men who died in the two World Wars, whose names appear on the two brass War Memorials in the church. In the first edition of "Cottisford Revisited", published in 1999, we were able to record the family backgrounds of eleven of those war dead, the only exception being H Farrer who had not been born in the Parish. We also included copies of photographs we had taken of seven of their memorials, mainly in France and Flanders. In the second edition, published early in 2008, we added a postscript giving the family background of H Farrer and a picture of his grave in France.

Figure 62

We also made an appeal in 1999 for photographs and other information about the men who had died. And we have more recently sought the help of the Commonwealth War Graves Commission in obtaining photographs of the memorials to the remaining four which are located in Greece, Jerusalem, Italy and Baghdad.

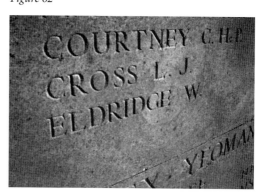

Figure 63

Through the courtesy of Michael Cross of Port Talbot we now have a picture (fig. 62) of the Cross family taken in about 1911 showing all seven of the sons, two of whom were killed within a few months of each other in 1917. There was also a daughter of the family, but it is thought that she was probably away "in service" at the time the picture was taken. The two boys who were killed in the war are in the middle of the back row – Allen Dennis Cross behind his mother and Leman John Cross behind his father. One of the other brothers standing in the back row, on the left, is William Cross who is known[134n] to have been so severely wounded in 1916 that he had to be invalided out of the service.

We also now have a picture of the inscription on the memorial to Leman John Cross (fig. 63) in the War Cemetery in Jerusalem. And a picture of Ernest Peverell's grave in Greece (fig. 64) where he had served in the Royal Field Artillery.

Unfortunately we have not yet been able to obtain a picture of the grave of the one remaining soldier from Cottisford who lost his life in the Great War – Sydney Gaskin. He died with many others in Turkish captivity after being taken prisoner with the survivors of the 1st Battalion, Oxfordshire & Buckinghamshire

Figure 64

Light Infantry[135n] after the disastrous siege of Kut, and was buried in a War Cemetery in Baghdad. Although presently inaccessible, this cemetery is said not to have been badly damaged in the recent conflict.

The one serviceman from Cottisford killed in the second World War was Ronald John Watts who served in the 5th Battalion, Grenadier Guards and was killed in February 1944 during the bitter fighting at Anzio in Italy. He, with all the others killed there, is commemorated in the Cassino War Cemetery.

A panoramic photograph (fig. 65) provided by the War Graves Commission of the Cassino cemetery shows the rugged terrain which enabled crack German troops here to hold up the Allied advance towards Rome for many months in 1944. Heavy casualties were suffered by both sides and the ancient monastery on the summit of Monte Cassino was eventually bombed into obliteration by the RAF and USAAF.

There is a tablet on which Ronald Watts is commemorated at Cassino (fig. 66). The Allies' achieved a successful landing at Anzio, intended to outflank the German defences at Cassino and hasten the advance on Rome. But the German's counter attacked strongly and the operation soon ground to a standstill as both sides dug in, and several difficult months were spent in

Figure 65

Figure 66

winter conditions that soon resembled the dreadful trench warfare of the Great War.

In April 2008 we first met Ron Collins of Tingewick. His mother had been Edith Agnes Watts before marriage, a sister of Ronald John Watts after whom she apparently named her son. Ron Collins kindly provided us with a picture of Ronald Watts in uniform, taken before he left the UK for service in North Africa and Italy (fig. 67). And we also learnt from him a significant fact – hitherto unrecorded.

In "Cottisford Revisited" we mentioned[136] that Ronald Watts had married Edna Mitchell at Taunton in 1942 before being posted overseas. But we had not known until we met Ron Collins that Edna bore a son, Michael Watts, who is today retired and living in Bradford on Avon. Later in 2008 we met Michael Watts and had a gratifying opportunity of talking with him about his father.

Michael has for many years shown intense interest in the father he never knew. Although surviving photographs and papers relating to Ronald Watts are scanty, they include one photograph of Edna with her baby son (fig. 68). And also a letter written to Edith Collins by a Guardsman R Smith describing the date and the exact location of the fierce engagement at Carroceto, in the Anzio beachhead, during which Ronald "went down fighting". Michael has visited and walked over this area, and has also been to the cemetery at Cassino and seen the commemorative tablet on which his father's name is inscribed.

It is clear from Guardsman Smith's letter that Edna Watts cannot have known that her husband was dead until many months had elapsed. Smith was taken prisoner and it was only after his return to the UK that the War Office asked him for information about Ronald Watts. Like so many others, Edna evidently endured much anxious waiting after being told that her husband was missing before the news of his death was confirmed to her.

Although this young soldier probably never saw his infant son, the fact that in adult life Michael has shown such interest in his father seems in some strange way to lessen slightly the sadness of Ronald Watts' death in action.

Figures 67 & 68

16. A DISTINGUISHED AIRMAN

In 1936 Cottisford House was purchased by a distinguished airman, Sir Robert Brooke-Popham. After a long career in the Royal Air Force, during which he had attained the rank of Air Chief Marshal, he was by then 57 years of age and had decided to retire into the country where he would be able to devote more of his time to hunting, which he greatly enjoyed. But it was not to be.

Almost immediately after he and his family had moved into Cottisford House early in 1937 Sir Robert received an invitation from the Secretary of State for the Colonies, Sir William Ormesby-Gore, to become Governor and Commander in Chief of Kenya, then a Crown Colony. Although this meant postponing his plans for retirement at Cottisford he accepted the offer. So he, his wife and two young children[137n] set sail on the British India Lines "SS Madura" for Kenya where they were to live for the next two and a half years, and Cottisford House was let to the Cottrell-Dormer family while they were away.

However, when the Second World War broke out in September 1939 Sir Robert straight away rejoined the RAF and a succession of important assignments delayed his effective retirement to Cottisford until 1942.

Sir Robert had been born in Suffolk in 1878 and baptised Henry Robert Moore Brooke. His father, Henry Brooke JP, was a country gentleman living at Wetheringsett Manor and his mother, Dulcibella Letitia formerly Moore, was the daughter of Rev Henry Moore, Rector of that Parish. Educated at Haileybury, he initially entered the army, graduating from Sandhurst in 1898 at the age of 20 as a Second Lieutenant in the Oxfordshire and Buckinghamshire Light Infantry. By 1904 he had been promoted to Captain.

In the same year he adopted the additional surname Popham by Royal Licence on inheriting an estate at West Bagborough in Somerset. This estate had long been in the ownership of the Pophams, a well-known West Country family, and his mother was a great granddaughter of Alexander Popham of that place. The inheritance came about through a cousin once removed of his mother, Susan Fenwick Bisset formerly Popham, who had died childless in 1903.

In 1910 he was selected for Staff College, but now began to show keen interest in his eventual speciality – aviation. It was only two years after Bleriot had flown across the English Channel (just) that Brooke-Popham started training to fly at Brooklands. In July 1911 he was granted (UK) Pilot's Licence No 108 and at that time the accompanying photograph (fig. 69) was taken for the Royal Aero Club. The following year he transferred to the pioneering Air Battalion of the Royal Engineers, and when that was converted into the Royal Flying Corps in 1912 he commanded one of the first squadrons.

Serving in France throughout the Great War, Brooke-Popham rose rapidly in rank. He became a Brigadier-General in 1916 and transferred into the new Royal Air Force in 1918, soon becoming an Air Commodore. He rose to the rank of

Figure 69

Air Vice Marshal in 1924, Air Marshal in 1931 and Air Chief Marshal in 1935. He was knighted in 1927.

Figure 70

As mentioned above, Sir Robert had inherited Bagborough House in 1904. When the Great War ended a large memorial (fig. 70) was erected outside the gate of the Parish church, which is adjacent to the house, recording not only those from the Parish who had been killed but all those who had served in the armed forces. Although the Royal Air Force had been created in 1918, its rank structure[138] and titles were not settled (after considerable debate) until August 1919. It can be seen that on this memorial Sir Robert, although in the RAF, was still referred to by his army rank of Brigadier General.

Sir Robert's career in the Services is well documented[139] and his entry in the Dictionary of National Biography provides a wide-ranging summary of his public life. He made a particularly noteworthy contribution to the early development of the RAF as the first Commandant of the RAF Staff College established in 1922 at Andover, a post he filled for five years. He later became Commandant of the Imperial Defence College. Early in the Second World War he was heavily involved in the setting up of the Empire Air Training Scheme in Canada and South Africa – an imaginative project without which the rapid expansion of the RAF during the war would not have been possible. On a personal level he evidently enjoyed a close relationship with Lord Trenchard – widely regarded as the "Father" of the RAF – who stood as Godfather to his son Philip at his baptism in 1928.

His long career in the Services showed him to be an unusually fine administrator and a forceful personality. His private life is much less well known.

It was not until 1926 that he married Opal Hugonin, 22 years his junior, who he had met at a Hunt Ball the previous year. Their two children, Diana and Philip, who accompanied them to Kenya, both remember the formalities and the fun of life at Government House in Nairobi.

In 1966 Sir Robert's substantial correspondence, with associated papers, was deposited by his widow at the Liddell Hart Centre for Military Archives in London. The papers relating to his Governorship of Kenya were then separated out and deposited at the Rhodes Library in Oxford. Most of these letters concern matters which were no doubt fairly routine in such Colonial postings – particularly the continual tension between settlers and the Africans and Europeans.

But the selection of a very experienced serviceman for the post of Commander in Chief had evidently been partly due to the Government's anxiety that Italy, after its very recent conquest of Abyssinia, might have further colonial ambitions in Africa. In a letter[140] to Ormsby-Gore in April 1938 Sir Robert gave a detailed account of the unexpected visit to Nairobi of Marshal Balbo, the Italian Governor General of Libya, piloting a three-engined S89 Savoia Marchetti aircraft.

At that time Marshal Balbo was a famous aviator. In 1933 he had led a formation of 24 Savoia Marchetti SM55 flying boats from Orbetello in Italy across the Atlantic to Chicago and back again. As a result of that feat the word "Balbo" had come into common usage[141] to describe any large formation of aircraft.

The two Brooke-Popham children still remember his visit. They were supposed to be in bed, but were allowed up to watch from a balcony upstairs as Marshal Balbo and his entourage moved with their hosts from the drawing room to the dining room of Government House.

There is one item in Sir Robert's official correspondence, a letter[142] from Ormsby-Gore in December 1937, which to 21st Century eyes looks bizarre in the extreme. In this letter Ormsby-Gore told Sir Robert, in the very strictest confidence, that the British Government was considering the possibility of handing over some of the British colonial territory in West Africa to Germany:

"I do recognise regretfully that if we are to re-establish better relations with Germany … and … move away from the present drift towards European conflagration, something will have to be done about German colonies … I have myself a dislike to transferring not merely territory but human beings from one rule to another against their will - but there it is. Germany somewhere in West Africa may well be part of the price of peace …".

The 1919 Treaty of Versailles had deprived Germany of all her African colonies and in 1937 this was thought to be particularly irksome to Herr Hitler. There is no record of what Sir Robert thought of this idea, though it may not have seemed quite so extraordinary to him as it does to the reader today. With the benefit of hindsight we can now be quite certain that the transfer of Nigeria, the Gambia or the Gold Coast to German rule in 1938 would not have placated Hitler or avoided the "conflagration" in Europe.

On the outbreak of war with Germany in September 1939 Sir Robert resigned his post as Governor and flew back to England where he immediately rejoined the RAF. The family followed him by air in December 1939 via Egypt and Malta, arriving at Croydon airport shortly before Sir Robert had to leave on a visit to Canada.

The evacuation of more than a million children from London was by then in full swing and Lady Brooke-Popham soon found herself with a very different household from the family home she must originally have envisaged. Cottisford House became a "War Nursery" accommodating up to 30 evacuee children ranging in age from two to five.

In "Cottisford Revisited" we mentioned this War Nursery briefly (on pages 52 and 53) and Donald Barker's time there as one of the evacuees. We can now, through the good offices of Sir Robert's son, Philip, reproduce here two pictures of some of the children (figs 71 & 72). The nursery came under the auspices of the Red Cross, who presumably provided the "nurse" in the

Figure 71

Figure 72

foreground in the picture of them having tea out of doors (fig. 71). The lady in the background of that picture is almost certainly Lady Brooke-Popham.

The small children who were evacuated to this War Nursery were fortunate. They received much kindness and had many happy memories of their time here.

In March 1944 Sir Robert revisited Kenya briefly and The East African Standard reported[143] him as saying that "Lady Brooke-Popham is as busy as ever … When I left home there were only twenty bombed-out children in the house – that is a small number for her – but I expect that since the bombing began again it has filled up. Anyway, we like to have them." The picture above shows two of the Red Cross staff with more than twenty of the children.

Lady Brooke-Popham ran a club for the girls and distributed very welcome presents to them at Christmas. Donald Barker, who lives today in Bicester, has kept in touch with many of them and arranges reunions at intervals which are attended by former evacuees who now live in Milton Keynes, London, Liverpool, Devon, Hampstead and Canada. One of them recently commented that when she eventually returned home at the age of nine it was a nasty change – going from the green of Oxfordshire to bombed-out Whitechapel, and meeting there the mother and siblings she scarcely knew.

All the bedrooms at Cottisford House, except one retained by Lady Brooke-Popham, were taken over for the War Nursery. When Diana and Philip returned for school holidays they had to sleep in a cottage at the back of the house. During this period they remember driving a pony and trap into Brackley to collect the rations from the International Stores.

The churchyard alongside Cottisford House contains memorials to two people with surnames unusual in the Parish who died within a few weeks of each other during the Second World War. Although these memorials are described[144] in our booklet "Cottisford MIs" published in 2006 it may not be obvious that they relate to close members of the Brooke-Popham family. The first is immediately to the east of the church porch, commemorating Edgar Hugonin, the father of Lady Brooke-Popham. He had died at Eastbourne on 17th May 1942. The second is nearby, close to the church path, and commemorates Dulcibella Mary Pooley, formerly Brooke. She was the only sister of Sir Robert, who had died at Hampstead on 23rd June 1942.

In 1942 Sir Robert was at last able to retire from the RAF and return to live at Cottisford, though he had not quite finished with the war and the services. He was appointed President of the Council of NAAFI. and also became a Captain in the local Home Guard. For many years he was Chairman of Cottisford Parish Meeting, and the Minutes of that body show him taking considerable pains over such local matters as the Parish's control over the allotments and playing field at Juniper Hill.

Figure 73, taken in about 1950, shows Sir Robert and Lady Brooke-Popham, together with Philip, relaxing over tea in the garden with two of their dogs. Another of their dogs made a vivid impression at the time on one small girl living in the village. Even today she still recalls the large, sandy coloured dog – a Rhodesian Ridgeback – "with the hair on the top of its back lying apparently the wrong way, i.e. towards its head".

Several other present-day residents of the area remember the generosity of the Brooke-Pophams, particularly the fetes and Christmas parties they organised. One particular memory recounted to us relates to the annual service in Cottisford Church on Armistice Day (November 11th). On those occasions Sir Robert sat in the chancel behind the screen, which in those days separated it from the nave, wearing all his decorations and medals (fig. 74).

Two of the servants at Cottisford House in those days were Charlie Patten and Percy Thredkil who worked both in the house and the gardens. Charlie Patten had been wounded in the Great War and had a wooden leg. It is said that when he visited the Fox Inn at Juniper Hill he had difficulty because the low ceiling forced him to stoop. Despite this handicap he nevertheless managed to ring the bell in the church on Sundays and a particular memory of him is that he had a parrot with a loud voice (and a wife with a loud laugh).

Figure 73

Figure 74

Figure 75

Figure 76

Like his father, son Philip was keen on flying, but his mother wanted him to serve in the Royal Navy. Both wishes were achieved when Philip was selected as one of a party of a dozen naval officers to attend a pilot's course at the RAF's Flying Training School at Syerston. He still today has a photograph of Cottisford House taken from his Miles Magister training aircraft. At the conclusion of the course at Syerston in June 1951 the "Inspecting Officer" was none other than Sir Robert, who had the great pleasure of presenting his son Philip with the "Wings" awarded to him as a pilot (fig. 75).

One of the last photographs of Sir Robert, (fig. 76), was taken on the morning of 2nd June 1953 on the steps of Cottisford House as he and Lady Brooke-Popham were leaving to attend the Coronation of the Queen in Westminster Abbey. He was by then a sick man, and died in October of that year in RAF Halton Hospital at Wendover.

His funeral in Bicester on 23rd October 1953 was an impressive final tribute to a much respected officer who had served in the RAF with great distinction. A contingent of 300 airmen[145] lined the funeral route to St Edburg's church and the six pall bearers accompanying the coffin comprised two Marshals of the Royal Air Force (one of them Viscount Portal, Chief of the Air Staff during the Second World War), three Air Chief Marshals and a Field Marshal. The church was packed with mourners ranging from senior officers of the services and the Lord Lieutenant of Oxfordshire, Lord Bicester from Tusmore House, to local dignitaries and many others who had known and worked with Sir Robert, including Charlie Patten and two other servants from Cottisford House. The private burial took place, as Sir Robert had wished, at West Bagborough, where the church and churchyard contain many memorials to members of the Popham family ranging back to the 18th Century.

With the exigencies of service, first in the army and then in the air force, Sir Robert had remained a bachelor for so many years that in 1922 he sold Bagborough House. His son Philip recalls that he seldom spoke of it, and that until his father's burial in 1953 he and his sister had been to West Bagborough only once, many years before, when they had been very small. In about 1959 the house came on the market again and Sir Robert's widow bought it back. When she died in 1983 she was buried at West Bagborough alongside Sir Robert.

Bagborough House is a fine building, on the edge of the Quantock Hills with wide views to the south and east, and Philip now lives there. Sir Robert would surely have been delighted if he had known that his family's strong link with the Pophams was to be restored in this way.

17. THE LAST VOYAGE OF MV JEDMOOR

The year 1941 was a grim one for this country in World War 2 with continuing air attacks on our cities, the loss of Greece and Crete (the last toeholds of our forces in Europe) and the German army driving ever deeper into the vast territories of our new-found Russian ally. The month of September was particularly sad for this Parish with the fatal crash of an aeroplane on Juniper Hill on 13th September, as already described in our booklet "Cottisford Revisited".

Earlier in that same week of September 1941 a further tragedy of a very different kind, which was destined to bring great sorrow to a daughter of the Parish, had been building up more than a thousand miles away on the cold grey waters of the North Atlantic[146,147]. Slow Convoy SC42, comprising 67 merchant ships carrying half a million tons of varied supplies for beleaguered Britain, had left the North American seaboard at Sydney, Nova Scotia on 30th August. After a week of atrocious weather, with two days almost hove-to in a howling gale, the convoy with a scanty escort of one destroyer and three corvettes was taking a north-easterly course past the southern tip of Greenland.

Amongst the merchant ships in that convoy was the *MV Jedmoor* (fig. 77), a 4,392 ton tramp built in 1928 at Sunderland for the Runciman company of Newcastle[148], on which Flora Thompson's younger son Peter was serving as Third Engineer[149]. The ship had already suffered[150] some war damage during an air raid on Belfast earlier in the year.

On her way south in June 1941 to take on a cargo of iron ore at Santos in Brazil there had been an alarm when she was sailing alone, just south of the equator, and the engine had coughed to a halt. The Chief Engineer soon diagnosed a blockage in the fuel supply line which would take several hours to clear and while the work was in progress, with the ship wallowing helpless in the water, the fighting top of a large warship appeared over the horizon. With German surface raiders known to be at large in the south Atlantic there was an anxious wait until the warship proved to be a British cruiser, *HMS Sheffield*, which swept past without pausing.

Blockage of that same oil feed pipe caused a much more serious alarm on 9th September

Figure 77

1941 when *Jedmoor* was sailing past the coast of Greenland in Convoy SC42. The engine again coughed to a halt and the rest of the convoy, together with all the escort, sailed past and was soon disappearing towards the horizon.

Ultra decrypts from Bletchley Park had already warned the Admiralty that a substantial "pack" of German U-boats was closing in on this convoy but attempts to re-route it were frustrated by continuing dreadful weather to the south. A single merchantman stopped and separated from the convoy was particularly vulnerable to attack and after two hours the lookouts on *Jedmoor* sighted the tracks of two torpedoes approaching, which fortunately missed. In fact, it is now known that no fewer than five torpedoes had been fired by *U-85*, all unsuccessful. On hearing news of this attack the Commander of the escort sent back two of the corvettes which kept *U-85* down until repairs had been completed and *Jedmoor* was able to rejoin the convoy.

Later that day the U-boats achieved their first sinking, when the *Empire Springbuck*, carrying steel and explosives, was hit by a salvo of torpedoes and blew up, sinking in two minutes with all her 42 crew. The next three days were a nightmare, with at least eight U-boats attacking the convoy, sometimes during the hours of darkness and sometimes in broad daylight. The twelve columns of merchant ships in the convoy covered more than 10 square miles (2,500 hectares) of ocean and at night the U-boats frequently surfaced within the convoy to attack. Ship after ship was torpedoed, and by the evening of 11th September a further 14 ships had been sunk with the loss of more than 200 merchant seamen.

This was one of the worst convoy disasters of WW2[151n] – reflected in Winston Churchill's later comment that:

> *"The only thing that ever really frightened me during the war was the U-boat peril"*

Apart from the loss of their vital cargoes, sinkings of merchant ships on this scale far exceeded any possible new construction, so that the merchant fleet on which the survival of this country depended was shrinking in size.

The convoy escort was hastily reinforced with more destroyers and corvettes from Iceland and by 14th September, as the convoy continued on its way at the slow speed of 7.5 knots, the carnage seemed to have abated – although a quarter of its ships had been lost. However, on 16th September, as the convoy was nearing St Kilda and the safety of home ports, a single U-boat struck one last blow. Unsuspected by the escort, *U-98* had worked its way submerged in the evening inside the convoy between the third and fourth columns of ships. Eventually *U-98* fired four torpedoes, aimed at the first four ships of the third column: only one of them scored a hit – on *Jedmoor*, the leading ship of the column. The torpedo hit the forward hold, tearing a jagged hole in the ship's side through which water poured rapidly and she began to go down by the head.

> *"As the Jedmoor's stern rose in the air, her propellers still threshing, there was a loud and ominous rumble as thousands of tons of iron ore in her holds shifted and ran towards the bows. One by one the watertight bulkheads of the holds collapsed under the weight, and the Jedmoor stood on her head as the whole of her cargo ended up in the fore part of the ship … (and) … she began her long descent to the bottom of the Atlantic".*

Because the *Jedmoor* sank so quickly only five of her crew of 36 were rescued. Flora Thompson's son Peter was not among them.

He is commemorated in four places. First, on the Merchant Navy memorial on Tower Hill in the City of London, close to the Headquarters of Trinity House, as illustrated on page 55 of "Cottisford Revisited": this is the impressive national memorial to all the 35,000 merchant seamen who were lost when more than 2,800 ships were sunk during WW2.

Secondly, on Dartmouth's War Memorial in a quiet corner of Royal Avenue Gardens where, on one of the gates, the British Legion's poppy emblem forms a striking accompaniment (fig. 78, p. 54). The strong call of the sea at Dartmouth is shown by the fact that more than half of the town's dead in WW2 served in the Royal Navy, the Royal Marines and the Merchant Navy.

Thirdly, on an unusual memorial in the small Church of St Petrox which stands next to the castle at the entrance to Dartmouth harbour. This church[152] serves the part of Dartmouth known as South Town. A large west gallery dating from the 17th Century was demolished in 1885 but some of the woodwork was later refurbished to provide a memorial to local men killed in both world wars. "Your Memory Hallowed In The Land You Loved" is inscribed across the top of this memorial and Peter Thompson's name is recorded on one of the small panels, as shown in figure 79.

Fourthly, at Flora Thompson's direction, on her own gravestone in Longcross Cemetery, Dartmouth (fig. 80).

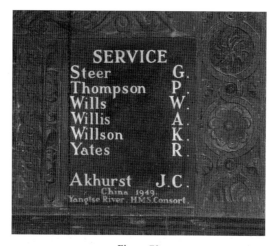

Figure 79

Figure 80

18. "LARK RISE" ON SCREEN AND STAGE

The title of Flora Thompson's trilogy "Lark Rise to Candleford" started to receive wide publicity in the winter of 2008 when a series of one-hour episodes under that name was screened by BBC TV on Sunday evenings. These episodes attracted a large audience of more than 6 million viewers. A second series under the same title followed in 2009, which attracted even more viewers, and a third series is being filmed at the time of writing for broadcasting during the winter of 2010.

The two series to date have had a strong cast and contained some excellent acting, but the so-called "adaption" for TV has been severe. The characers of some of the main participants have been radically altered, and several of the episodes have borne little resemblance to anything that was recorded in the books. For example, the mere suggestion that the daughter of Flora's authoritarian Rector, Mr Ellison, might have married a postman in the late 19th Century must surely have caused the Rev Charles Sawkins Harrison to turn in his grave!

As a result, some Flora Thompson enthusiasts are luke-warm, or even hostile, to these series. Nevertheless, they have proved to be popular viewing, and do have the merit of providing a regular Sunday evening show mercifully free of drama-filled hospitals, cops and robbers, or smut.

And there has been one important incidental benefit. Penguin have produced a reprint[153] (fig. 81, p.47) in their Modern Classics series with a picture of Olivia Hallinan, who takes the part of Flora/Laura in the TV series, on the front cover which has evidently sold well. As a result, new readers have been introduced to the books who, as soon as they begin reading "Lark Rise", discover that the first two BBC series have depicted almost nothing of Flora Thompson's childhood. As a result, that first book – which is the most factual and important of the trilogy – has been introduced to a wider audience, many of whom have greatly enjoyed the books and become enthusiasts.

A much closer interpretation of the books than the TV series is provided by Keith Dewhurst's two plays "Lark Rise"[154] and Candleford"[155], commissioned by the National Theatre in 1978 and 1979. After highly successful runs at the Cottesloe Theatre, with music provided by the Albion Band, they have been widely performed by amateur groups – particularly in Oxfordshire and adjacent parts of Buckinghamshire, but also in Hampshire where Flora Thompson lived for many years after her marriage. These plays, particularly "Lark Rise", retain one of the essential underlying themes of the books – resilience in the face of rural poverty – which has been largely lost in the BBC's TV version.

On Saturday, 26th May 2007, to mark the 60th anniversary of Flora Thompson's death, there was a performance of the play "Lark Rise" on the playing field at Juniper Hill. Substantial grants had been obtained from the National Lottery and Cherwell District Council so that this could take place under cover in a large marquee. The performance was given by the Garsington and Wheatley Barnstormers with music by the Black Fox band.

This was the first-ever performance in Flora Thompson's birthplace and had the appropriate title "Lark Rise at Lark Rise". All 312 seats were sold several weeks in advance and a cosmopolitan audience included people from many parts of the UK, plus enthusiasts from the USA, South Africa, Canada and Japan – the last of these being a lady[156n] who has translated "Lark Rise" into Japanese. Hugo Brunner, then Lord Lieutenant of Oxfordshire, was there; the late

Grace Broughton, last teacher at Cottisford School before it closed in 1968 was there; and the playright Keith Dewhurst was there.

The performance of the play was excellent (fig. 82). It took place in the afternoon, after which members of the audience were able to walk round the Rise and visit the garden of the "End House" at which Flora spent her childhood years. It was the first time that Keith Dewhurst had visited Juniper Hill since 1978. Afterwards, he sent us an appreciative message in which he summed up the hamlet in just a few well-chosen words "Despite everything the place itself retains its isolated feeling – a little world still".

During the evening of the performance, a hog roast was held for Parishioners and invited guests at the conclusion of which snuff was served – in memory of Queenie[157]. And the following day a well-attended memorial service was held in Cottisford Church. There were several readings from "Lark Rise", including a reminder from the then Rector, Ricky Yates, of that memorable occasion when Flora's Rev Ellison was so carried away with indignation after an election in which some Parishioners were suspected of having voted for the Liberal party, that he actually swore from the pulpit[158].

The brass War Memorial in the church provides an ever-present reminder of the deep sadness of the final paragraph[159] of "Lark Rise" in which Flora records that in the Great War "eleven out of that tiny community never came back", amongst them her dearly loved brother, Edwin Timms. One of the great strengths of Keith Dewhurst's play "Lark Rise" is the sensitive and moving way in which that terrible event is foretold (fig. 83).

Figures 82 and 83

19. A TRUE DAUGHTER OF JUNIPER HILL

This booklet about Cottisford Parish has covered a wide span of history and touched on the lives of many former Parishioners, some well-to-do, some comfortably off and many on the fringes of poverty. We have adopted a more-or-less chronological arrangement but one name has appeared repeatedly in several of the chapters – that of Flora Thompson, formerly Timms. She and her books are referred to in our Introduction and then again in Chapters 2, 9, 11, 13, 14, 17 and 18.

Her importance is underlined by the fact that she is the only native of the Parish to have gained a place in the Dictionary of National Biography for at least 400 years. Many reviewers of her books have praised the exceptional quality of her writing which, after limited formal education, blossomed in later life. As a child she was unusually perceptive. During those formative years she stored away a host of memories which she then recalled much later in life and set down in the books which are largely autobiographical. By the time she drafted the first of the articles which were later brought together in "Lark Rise" she had already reached middle age: 40 years had elapsed since she had left Juniper Hill to start work in the village Post Office at Fringford 2½ miles (4 km) away.

In addition to her perceptiveness and excellent memory, she was also a very accomplished wordsmith. Many of her phrases are richly evocative. To mention but one memorable phrase, we have already quoted in Chapter 13 her description of the time when the Rise "stood in a wide expanse of open heath, with juniper bushes and furze thickets and close, springy, rabbit-bitten turf".

And there is another of Flora Thompson's qualities which is worthy of emphasis. Just like many of the other natives of Juniper Hill of whom she wrote, she did not flinch. Reading her books one appreciates her lightness of touch and warm-hearted approach to life. But it might well have been different. Her personal experience of life had been anything but serene and could so easily have led to bitterness.

Flora was born into a poorly off family and the most important man in her early years – her father, Albert Timms – was a moody, unpopular individual with a chip on his shoulder, who drank. The second important man in her life – her husband, John Thompson – was a strait-laced individual who for many years gave her no encouragement whatever in the writing to which she was so devoted.

Added to these adversities, she suffered two personal tragedies which hit her hard. First during the Great War when, after many months of anxiety about her much-loved younger brother Edwin serving at the front in Flanders, one of her own recent letters to him was returned amongst the regular daily post with the chilling words "Killed in action" written on the envelope. Flora was a sensitive soul, and her daughter said many years later that[160] "she was quite simply heartbroken" by this news.

And later in life, during the Second World War, when her younger son Peter was killed in an Atlantic convoy. We have included in Chapter 17 a short description of the loss of the *MV Jedmoor* because, even for those who lived through that conflict, the gravity of the U-boat peril and the horrors it created were largely hidden[161n].

Peter Thompson had loved the sea. He had been ten when the family moved to Dartmouth and throughout his childhood accompanied his father to sea in his dingy "Sea Mew" whenever he could. He had been apprenticed as a ship's engineer at the age of 17 and had joined the Merchant Navy early in the Second World War. Of his death Flora wrote in a personal letter[162] "He was our youngest, a latecomer and tenderly loved. That there are thousands of mothers and wives suffering as I am only seems to make it harder to bear".

She never fully recovered her health after Peter's death.

Yet, despite all these setbacks and sorrows, Flora's books remain relaxed and sunny. To the outside world she remained a true daughter of Juniper Hill – she did not flinch[163n].

APPENDIX A:
CHILDHOOD MEMORIES OF THE RECTORY DURING THE 1920s AND 1930s

These reminiscences were written in 1987 by the late Mrs Joan Cottrell (formerly Wallis), who had been baptised here in 1917, though born at Burnley, a granddaughter of Rev Statham the rector of Cottisford and Hardwick from 1912 to 1947. She wrote them originally for her niece, Mrs Heather Thorn, but kindly agreed in 2008 to their use in this booklet. Like Flora Thompson's "Lark Rise", they provide a personal glimpse of daily life in the Parish through the eyes of a child. Although, in this case, recording life in one of the more privileged households, there are many striking contrasts with today.

I have often tried to think out how to describe the spell that Cottisford cast over me, and all my family. I loved it all dearly and was entirely happy there and have thought of it with a real heartache many times since Grandpa died. The main things were, I think, its orderliness and security – the days went by without great events but in much contentment and, for us children, complete freedom to roam about out of doors.

The house itself was very pleasant, built of soft red brick partly covered with ivy. One entered through a narrow glassed-in porch through an arch into the hall, off which led the study, the main staircase, the conservatory and a passage through to the kitchen shut off by the traditional baize-covered door which squeaked and thumped on opening and closing. There was a big club fender at the hall fire place. On Sundays Grandpa would robe there and stand saying his preliminary prayers into his bowler hat before going across the road to the church where we would sit – a little embarrassed – alongside him in the chancel choir stall while blue-jowled Charley James rang the two ding-dong bells and Ethel Fletcher played the little organ.

Ethel was the backbone of the household. She was cook, housekeeper, curate (unpaid) and companion and ran the house quietly and efficiently with one or two women from the village to help. Grandpa eventually became infirm and practically blind (he was 88 when he died) and it was marvellous how she looked after him and kept the house and the church going. All this in a house with no gas or electricity and no running water apart from what was pumped up daily from the two wells. In the scullery there was a pump at the stone sink, and another in the downstairs cloakroom, where old Dale the gardener used to come every evening to pump the tank full. One of my memories is of the "clump, thump" of the pump as he worked away. The water was heated by an old black range in the kitchen and fed to the two bathrooms upstairs. For kitchen use, the range had a tank at one side with a tap.

Part of Cottisford's charm was the lamplight. Lamps and candles were kept on a ledge in the wall half-way up the back stairs out of the kitchen, cleaned and filled every morning ready for Ethel to bring them into whichever room we were sitting in in the evening. Candles, of course, to go to bed with. And brass jugs of hot water came up in the morning to wash with.

In very hot summers the wells would run dry and I imagine that water was brought round in tankers. Then one winter the kitchen range cracked and could be used neither for water nor for cooking and Ethel had to make do with paraffin cookers. It must have been bitterly cold in the winter, especially in the kitchen with its red-tiled floor (worn into humps and hollows) and the stone floored scullery, but we never went to stay then. I suppose it must have rained sometimes when we were there, but I can only remember it pattering on the corrugated iron roof of the barn, never being out in it.

The drawing room had bay french windows opening out onto the lawn. This was a lovely room, very quiet and peaceful, and very snug in the evenings when Ethel brought the lamp in and drew down the long cherry-red blinds at the windows. There was a handsome tiled fireplace with folding tiled shutters which could be drawn across the barred grate. The fire was only lit on Sundays when we had tea there. Grandpa's nicest china was there, some on the mantelpiece and some in a bow-fronted china cabinet. There was a little escritoire and a small black wood grand piano with the royal crest carved on the lid which was reputed to have come from Buckingham Palace. Grandpa was a great one for going to sales and no doubt picked up some of the nice things there.

On the opposite side of the passage was the stone-floored cloakroom where Dale pumped the water, then the dining room with a hatch to the kitchen, and more french windows into the orchard part of the garden. This was another nice room. It looked up the road to the village and to a pond where the cart horses were brought down to drink.

Down two or three steps into the kitchen then, with its pine scrubbed table under which was a big footstool occupied by Fluff, Granny's big ginger Persian cat, which I was not too keen on.

There was a big larder off, then into the scullery with another cool larder, the sink and pump, and out into a passage towards the barn. One of my jobs was cleaning the knives with one of those big circular machines with slots in the top, into which one pushed the knives (steel and very sharp) and then turned the handle to brush and polish them with accompanying rumbles from something loose inside. That's the only chore I remember doing, perhaps also laying and clearing the dining table.

Upstairs ("Don't think I'm being impolite, gentlemen always go upstairs first" said Grandpa, going ahead of me once) up three steps to one room, along the passage to the Blue room, then another study opposite the bathroom and two smaller bedrooms, then the main bedroom with its own bathroom opening off.

The upstairs study was used to sit in on weekday evenings, being small and cosy. It had a fireplace with a hob either side with a tub of paper spills, most of which Grandpa would use up puffing and re-lighting his pipe. He had an organ up there too and would often play for a while and we would hear the owls hooting across the lawn. Occasionally bats would fly into the bedroom. I handled one once the boys had caught, a nice little pipistrelle I think, but it bit me.

The grounds were a delight, with two glebe fields to one side, with a stream running through to make a pond, then a sluice gate to flow away past the bottom of the kitchen garden and a tributary running through the further field – smelling of wild mint, with occasional snakes. Grass-snakes would swim across the pond and once an adder curled up in the sun, which sadly had to be killed. Not many fish in the pond, though the boys did catch a pike once. Below the sluice the stream was silted up and we used to balance across it using two chairs from the barn, which had wooden chairs and benches for Parish occasions.

On one side of the house was a small orchard consisting of old mossy leaning apple trees and a quince tree and on the other a lawn with two walnut trees, raided by grey squirrels and on the far side some scraggy pine trees where the owls used to sit and hoot at night. Then through a thick yew hedge to the big kitchen-garden its paths lined with little box hedges. Over the wall were several pig-sties, by then beginning to fall into ruin.

There was a row of little out-houses across the tiled path up to the back door, where were kept coal, the mangle and a big drum of paraffin. The barn backed onto these with, at the field end of it, the coach house and stable with a loft above. It seems that I cried a great deal as a baby and when the household could stand it no longer would be wheeled into the barn to go off to sleep.

It was a wonderful place for natural history. I remember staying there once at Maytime and putting my head out of the window to listen to the dawn chorus, and finding it almost a barrage of sound, like a waterfall. The Heath was our favourite haunt, a huge area of scrub and bracken and beechwoods from the edge of which we could see Tusmore House, where Grandpa would occasionally walk over to play chess with Lord Effingham. We found long-tailed tit's nests in the blackthorn thickets, adders and grass snakes, foxes and sadly an owl caught in a pole-trap and hanging wretchedly by its trapped feet. Thank goodness they've long been illegal. We found a vixen shot one day and not far off three little fox-cubs at the mouth of her burrow. They were very pretty, a smoky blue colour with blue eyes and we managed to catch one and took it home, but Granny threw up her hands and said "Take it away"! I think we tried to keep it but the poor thing died, as the others in the burrow must have.

I realise that I've said little about Granny – I suppose Ethel had more dealings with us. Latterly, Granny became very confused, but she was a very kind person and did a lot for the women of the village. When going out she wore a veil, and I believe would walk the five miles to Brackley and back again to shop. After she died in 1933 my father found a choir screen for Grandpa to put in Cottisford church in her memory. It has now been moved to the west end where it makes a small right-angled enclosure for a tiny vestry.

On Sundays when Grandpa had duty at his other church (at Hardwick), Cox would come with his pony and little tub governess trap and take us clopping along on the gravelly roads. After church we would go across the farm-yard to Mr Hiron's farm-house for a chat. Later, Cox acquired a taxi, not so much fun but still a symbol of opulence to me – he would come to Finmere station to meet us

Figure 84

when we travelled by train. My father joined us sometimes if we were there when he had finished his three-week stint at Oxford marking exam papers.

A little more about the house. The downstairs study was rarely used, rather a cold room said to have another well under the table in the middle of the room. The conservatory (gone now) opened off the hall and had pot-plants in, begonias mostly. Grandpa would plant for us a copper coin and – lo and behold – in the morning it had turned to silver!

I have a small leather-bound Bible in a leather case inscribed "Sherard M Statham, from his father, September 22nd 1877". This would be the year he was 18, possible a gift before going up to Cambridge. It had obviously been much read as there are quite a few pencil marks against the verses, mostly in the Old Testament and there mostly in the Psalms. "Wonderful for comfort, Joan, wonderful for comfort" he said to me once.

Well there's Cottisford for you – nice to share it.

Joan Cottrell

Rev Statham is the subject of a chapter "A long-serving Rector" in "Cottisford Revisited".
A photograph of Ethel Fletcher can be found on page 44 of that booklet, together with more details of her life.

APPENDIX B:
A CHILDHOOD MEMORY OF A FORMER COTTISFORD ROUSBY IN ABOUT 1942

These reminiscences were written in 2008 by Mrs Colette Allen of Bedford: her mother, Gladys Ellen Butler, had been a Rousby by birth.

Living in Sutton Coldfield during the war was not very exciting for a young girl. Out of the blue my mother received an invitation to lunch from a great great aunt, Josephine Worley (formerly Rousby), who lived in Stoney Stratford (fig. 85).

My mother was asked to bring one of her children with her. I had three brothers. My mother thought about this and decided to take the best-behaved of us: to my delight I was chosen. I really was a bit of a tomboy with having three brothers, but still I passed the test.

We were to be collected from Wolverton Station by Josephine Worley's chauffeur, which duly happened, and taken to the big house for lunch. I was very impressed by everything and my table manners were impeccable. My most vivid memories of the day are of the beauty of the house and garden. She showed us many things amongst which were two or three old musical boxes – quite large – which to me as a young girl were magical! Also I remember being shown some photographs, obviously of members of the family, in small oval frames, which when turned over showed locks of hair either curled or plaited.

She was a delightful old lady. I think it must have been from her that we received copies of several photographs and other mementos relating to the Cottisford Rousbys which we still retain. We had a most enjoyable time and after tea were returned to Wolverton Station by her chauffeur.

Many, many, years on I still treasure that childhood memory.

Apart from the photograph of Josephine Worley shown here, the pictures of Captain Arthur Rousby and of his grave in Shanghai (in Chapter 11 – "The Rousby Era") are amongst the relics evidently passed on by Josephine Worley to Gladys Butler. Josephine Worley was the sister of E R K Rousby and, under his Will, received the bulk of his estate after his death in 1928. She lived on to the ripe old age of 94. Her Will, made in 1947, shows that she was living at Stratford House, Stoney Stratford and left "effects" of £16,723. Amongst a wide range of bequests she gave £50 to Gladys Butler, which seems to confirm that Colette's table manners during their only meeting must, indeed, have been up to standard!

Figure 85

APPENDIX C:
ACCOUNTS RELATING TO REV CHARLES COTTON'S
FUNERAL ON 21ST MARCH 1799

The two main surviving accounts are reproduced here (figs. 86 & 87), together with transcripts. These cover what would be known today as Undertakers' services. Short excerpts of other accounts are reproduced in Chapter 7 covering the preparation of the brick grave at Cottisford and the provision of the coffin.

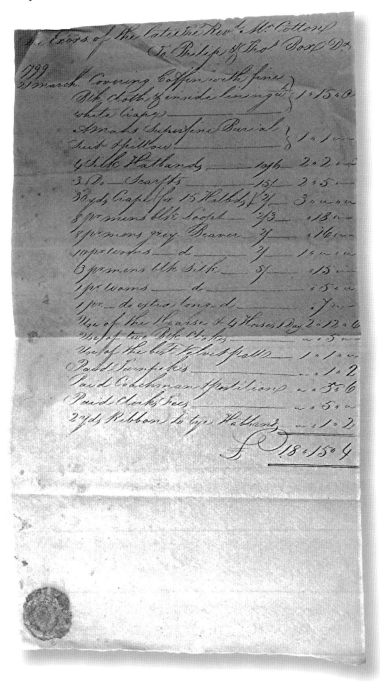

Figure 86

The Exors of the late The Revd Mr Cotton
To Philip & Thos Box Dr

1799

21 March	Covering Coffin with fine Blk cloth & inside lining wth white Crape		1 = 15 = 0
	A Mans Superfine Burial Suit and pillow		1 = 1 = 0
	4 Silk Hatbands	10/6	2 = 2 = 0
	3 do Scarffs	15/-	2 = 5 = 0
	30 yds Crape (for 15 Hatbands)	2/-	3 = 0 = 0
	8 pr mens blk Loops	2/3	8 = 0
	8 pr mens grey Beaver	2/-	16 = 0
	10 pr Woms do	2/-	1 = 0 = 0
	3 pr mens blk Silk	5/-	15 = 0
	1 pr Woms do		5 = 0
	1 pr do extra long		7 = 0
	Use of the Hearse and 4 Horses 1 Day		2 = 12 = 6
	Use of 2 Blk Cloaks		5 = 0
	Use of the best Velvet Pall		1 = 1 = 0
	Paid Turnpikes		1 = 2
	Paid Coachman & Postilion		5 = 6
	Paid Clerks Fees		5 = 0
	2 yds Ribbon to tye Hatbands		1 = 2
			£18 = 15 = 4

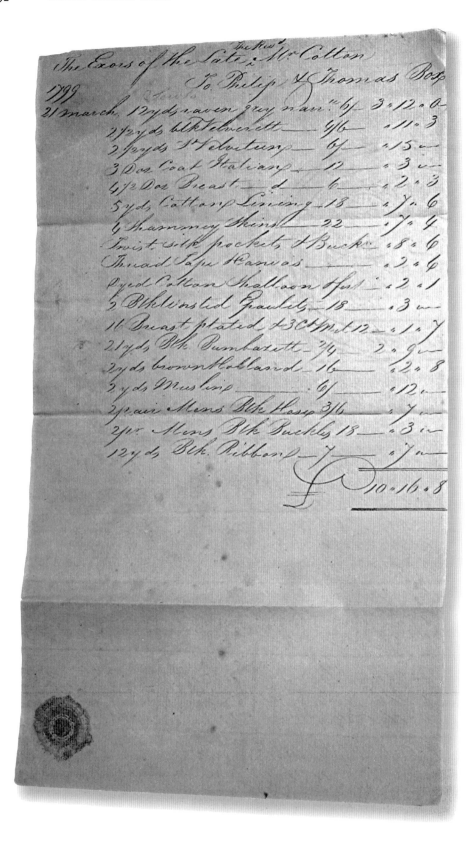

Figure 87

The Exors of the late The Revd Mr Cotton
To Philip & Thomas Box

1799

21 March	12 yds raven grey nan	6/-		3 =	12 =	0
	2 ½ yds blk Velverett	4/6			11 =	3
	2 ½ yds do Velveteen	6/-			15 =	0
	3 Doz Coat Italian	1d			3 =	0
	4 ½ Doz breast do	6d			2 =	3
	5 yds Cottony Lining	18			7 =	6
	4 Shammy Skins	22			7 =	4
	Twist silk pockets & Buckm				8 =	6
	Thread Tape/Canvas				2 =	6
	Dyed Cotton Shalloon and firs				2 =	1
	2 Blk Worsted Epaulets	18			3 =	-
	11 Breast plated & 3 Ctfm at	12			1 =	7
	21 yds Blk Bumbarett	2/4		2 =	9 =	0
	2 yds brown Holland	16			2 =	8
	2 yds Musling	6/-			12 =	0
	2 pair Mens Blk Hoses	3/6			7 =	0
	2 pr Mens Blk Buckles	18			3 =	0
	12 yds Blk Ribbon	7			7 =	0
				£10 =	16 =	8

APPENDIX D:
THE SEVEN LEDGER STONES

As described and illustrated in Chapter 7, there are seven large ledger stones immediately outside the east (chancel) end of the church. They all commemorate members of the Cotton family (or their spouses) who, although living outside the Parish, were buried here because of their close connection with the Lord family, formerly of Cottisford House. The inscriptions on these stones were transcribed and recorded in our booklet "Cottisford MIs" published in 2006.

However, since then, two sources of written information have complicated our understanding of this group of stones. The first of these sources is Blomfield's History of the Parish of Upper Heyford published in 1892. Shuckburgh Cotton, who had married Anne the eldest surviving daughter of Lawrence Lord (2) here in 1732, had been Rector of both Upper Heyford and Newton Purcell. Blomfield recorded (on page 54 of that publication) that he vacated the rectory at Heyford in 1734 and then resided in Newton Purcell up to the time of his death in 1762 "and was buried there". That is clearly a slip on the part of Blomfield. A footnote refers to Cottisford Church Register, in which the burial of Shuckburgh Cotton here was correctly recorded, as confirmed by the inscription on the oldest of the seven ledger stones.

On the same page Blomfield refers to Rev Charles Cotton, the eldest surviving son of Shuckburgh Cotton who had succeeded him as Rector of Heyford, as being buried in the churchyard at Cottisford in 1799 "among the graves of his family at the east end of the church". That is correct, but Blomfield then lists seven other members of that family, two of whom are not recorded on any of the seven ledger stones. These missing names being Charles Cotton (son of Charles) in 1774 and Mary Cotton (from Tingewick) in 1798.

Both of those burials are recorded in Cottisford Burial Register. And the burial of Miss Mary Cotton in October 1798 is confirmed by two of the accounts reproduced in Chapter 7. One relates to "A Coffin for Miss Mary Cotton" in that month; and the other is for "Making Brick Grave for Miss Molly Cotton at Cottsford" at the same time. One ledger stone now commemorates Elizabeth Cotton in 1795 and Charles Cotton in 1799, though there are accounts for two brick graves being prepared here separately for them in those years: and another discrepancy is that the name of Charles Cotton appears first on the stone although he was buried second.

This is puzzling – the ledger stones surviving do not fully correspond with either Blomfield's list or the Tingewick accounts. The latter must, surely, have been correct as they were contemporary. The only possible explanation we can suggest is prompted by Blomfield's statement (in a footnote on page 22 of his book on Cottisford) that these ledger stones were "restored a few years ago by Rev Cotton Risley". Perhaps one or more of the stones had by then collapsed and alterations had to be made to them then.

It may never be possible to resolve the inconsistencies. For the benefit of anyone interested in the burials of these descendants of the Lord family we list below what appear to be the facts. For ease of reference the ledger stones have been numbered here from south to north. They are in two rows, Nos 1–5 near the church and 6–7 immediately to the east of them.

Rev Shuckburgh Cotton was buried here on 26th September 1762 and is commemorated on ledger stone No 1

His wife Anne, formerly Lord, was buried here on 13th November 1774 and is commemo-rated on ledger stone No 2

As mentioned in Chapter 7, they had nine children. The list below shows that all except one of them were brought to Cottisford for burial:

Holford Cotton baptised 16th August 1733 was buried here (aged 6) on 25th May 1740. No memorial.

Charles Cotton baptised 18th March 1736 was buried here on 25th March 1799 and is com-memorated on ledger stone No 7

Anne Cotton baptised 19th May 1739 was buried here (unmarried) on 7th August 1768 and is commemorated on ledger stone No 3

Elizabeth Cotton baptised 4th July 1741 was buried here (unmarried) on 22nd January 1795 and is commemorated with her brother Charles on ledger stone No 7 although a separate brick grave had been prepared for her. Although she was buried first, her inscription comes second

Mary Cotton baptised 8th February 1743 was buried here (unmarried) on 31st October 1798. No memorial, but included on Blomfield's list and a brick grave was prepared for her

Lydia Cotton baptised 28th October 1744 was married to Rev George James Sale, buried here on 6th February 1787 and is commemorated on ledger stone No 4. Not included in Blomfield's list

Holford Cotton baptised 31st May 1746 was not buried here but at Adderbury on 24th August 1822

Alicia Cotton baptised 11th May 1749 was buried here (aged 3 weeks) on 7th June 1749. No memorial.

Shuckburgh Cotton baptised 24th May 1750 was buried here (aged 1 week) on 2nd June 1750. No memorial.

In addition to the above children of Shuckburgh and Anne Cotton, their grandson Charles, son of Charles, was buried here on 6th April 1774. No memorial, but included on Blomfield's list.

Lydia Sale's husband George James Sale was buried here on 4th June 1773 and is commemo-rated on ledger stone No 5. Not included on Blomfield's list

Charles Cotton's wife Mary was buried here on 19th February 1774 and is commemorated on ledger stone No 6

The absence of any memorials to the young children buried here is not unusual.

All these burials, like those of other members of the Lord family under the chancel, dem-onstrate the strong attachment of this family to the Parish long after they had ceased to live here.

REFERENCES AND NOTES

References are marked in the text by a small superscript, thus [13]. Notes supplementary to the text are similarly marked but with the letter "n" added, thus [17n].

To keep this list to a reasonable length we have not provided references to self-evident information which can readily be traced from the details given, such as the many Census enumerator's returns covered particularly in Chapter 14. This information can be retrieved at the touch of a key from one of several family history sites on the Internet, such as "Ancestry UK". The Clergy of the Church of England Database (CCEd) provides details on the web of clergy 1540–1835 and Crockford's Clerical Directory gives later details.

All references to "Lark Rise to Candleford", or any of the individual books in the trilogy, are to the Penguin film and TV tie-in edition published in 2008 (with a picture of Olivia Hallinan on the front cover).

Chapter 1

1. Thompson F J, "Over to Candleford", Chapter XVI, p. 256

2. Thompson F J, "Lark Rise", Chapter I, p. 17

3. Ibid. p. 18

4. Jones A, "A thousand years of the English Parish", Windrush Press, Gloucestershire, 2000, p. 15

5. Flaxman Ted & Joan, "Cottisford Revisited", second edition, 2008

Chapter 2

6n. In a thought-provoking article published in "Victorian Studies", Vol 29, 1985/6, pp. 7–34, Barbara English of the University of Hull picks out some elements of "Lark Rise" which can be shown to be inaccurate and others where uncomfortable facts are omitted – notably any mention of the deaths of Flora's own siblings. In our view these criticisms do not significantly reduce the value of "Lark Rise" as a perceptive piece of social history. In describing the book we have adopted the phrase "Autobiographical novel", which is in widespread use. The auto-biographical content of the book far outweighs the novel and the passages we quote from the book appear to us to reflect fact rather than fiction.

7. Thompson F J, "Lark Rise", Chapter XV, p. 247

8. Tucker Pat, "Let's look at Launton", Launton Historical Society, second edition, 2003, pp. 9 & 39

9. Blomfield Rev J C, "History of the present Deanery of Bicester, Oxon", Parker & Co, Oxford and London, 1882

10. Blomfield Rev J C, "The History of Bicester – Its Town and Priory", Smith and Pankhurst, Bicester, 1884

11. Blomfield Rev J C, "History of Cottisford, Hardwick and Tusmore", J W Arrowsmith, Bristol, 1857

12. Oxfordshire Record Society, Parochial Collections made by Anthony Wood and Richard

Rawlinson, Volume 1, 1920, p. 102

13. "A history of Oxfordshire – Ploughley Hundred", Victoria County History, Volume VI, Oxford University Press, 1959

14. Ibid. pp. 107 & 108

15. "The Victoria History of the County of Oxfordshire", Volume I, 1939, reprinted 1970 by Dawsons, London, pp. 384 & 427

16. Stephens W B, "Sources for English local history", Phillimore, 1994, pp. 47–48

17n. Although little is known for certain about the history of the Parish before the Norman conquest it has been suggested that the stonework of the present nave of St Mary's church may largely consist of the remains of a Saxon church which is known to have existed at the time of the conquest. This suggestion is based on (a) the dimensions of the nave and (b) the form of some of the quoins used in its construction. It seems unlikely that this will ever be either proved or disproved. See Milnes-Walker H, "A Saxon church at Cottisford ?", Oxoniensis, Vol XLIII, 1978, pp. 255 & 256

Chapter 3

18. "Alumni Oxonienses 1500–1714", Volume III, James Parker, Oxford, 1891, p. 938

19. "The Statutes at large from 1st Edward IV to end of Elizabeth", Volume the Second, MDC-CLXX pp. 614–615, "Anno XVIII Reginae Elizabethae CAP VI", 1576, Maintenance of the Colleges in the Universities, and of Winchester and Eaton

20. "A history of Oxfordshire – Ploughley Hundred", Victoria County History, Volume VI, Oxford University Press, 1959, p. 111

21. Romulus Press: Biography Database 1680–1830

22. "Alumni Oxonienses 1715–1886", III, Parker & Co, Oxford, 1888, pp. 872 & 873

23. Bradney Sir Joseph, "History of Monmouthshire", Vol III Part 2, The Hundred of Usk, 1923, reprinted 1993, p. 177

24n. Flaxman Ted & Joan, "Cottisford MIs", 2006, pp. 18 & 23. The Victoria History of Oxfordshire Volume 6 page 144 refers to inscriptions in Fritwell church to "two daughters of Laurence Lord (early 18th cent.) which have disappeared". The Latin inscription to Elizabeth Lord baptised and buried at Cottisford in 1703 describes her as the "first born daughter of Lawrence Lord Esq", so it seems that these must have been daughters of Lawrence Lord (1).

25n. The entry for Robert Lord, son of Lawrence Lord of Cottisford, in "Alumni Oxonienses" 1715–1886 p. 873 states that he was minister of a Dissenting Protestant chapel in Knutsford, Cheshire and died in 1801. That is incorrect. The Rev Robert Lord at Knutsford was a different person who had been born at Dean in Lancashire and obtained his MA at Glasgow University – a well known source of dissenting ministers – in 1737.

26. Bradney Sir Joseph, "History of Monmouthshire", Vol III Part 2, The Hundred of Usk 1923, reprinted 1993, p. 178

Chapter 4

27. Bradney Sir Joseph, "History of Monmouthshire", Vol III Part 2, The Hundred of Usk, 1923, reprinted 1993, pp. 178 & 180

28. Ibid. p. 183

29n. Newman John, "The buildings of Wales, Gwent/Monmouthshire", Penguin Books/University of Wales Press, 2000, p. 259. Bradney's book contains on page 174 a picture by Hando, the illustrator, of Kemys Manor which is impossible to reconcile with the appearance of the house today.

Chapter 5

30. Flaxman Ted & Joan, "Cottisford MIs", 2006, p. 23

31n. This substantial archive from the office of Messrs Hearne, Solicitors of Buckingham, is currently in the possession of Tingewick Historical Society and was kindly made available to us for study. We refer to it throughout as the "Hearne Archive". No catalogue has yet been prepared of individual items but we have provided the Society with copies of the numbered digital photos we have taken of those referred to in Chapters 5 and 7. For ease of reference we have generally included below the relevant photo numbers. There is one exception, which is described in Reference 33n below.

32. Bradney Sir Joseph, "History of Monmouthshire", Vol III Part 2, The Hundred of Usk, 1923, reprinted 1993, Pedigree of the families of Cotton and Risley, p. 180

33n. Amongst the Hearne Archive referred to above in Note 31n is a bulky draft "Abstract of Title to the sevl parts and shares of an Estate at Souldern in the County of Oxon (formerly Lord's)". This comprises 23 large sheets written on both sides and so heavily folded as to be very difficult to photograph. It is useful in summarising many different documents and in revealing the indebtedness of Allen Lord to his mother at the time of his decease in 1771.

34. Hearne Archive. A summary of the amounts due to several beneficiaries from the £2,300 proceeds of sale for the Souldern lands, Photo 0730

35. Ibid. Letter from Charles Heynes to Mr Hearne dated 3rd June 1824, Photo 0633

Chapter 6

36. "Alumni Oxonienses 1500–1714", Volume IV, James Parker, Oxford, 1891, p. 1596

37n. Much of the original research into the four letters was carried out by Sue Baxter, then of Buckinghamshire Record Office. Since leaving the Record Office and setting up as an independent archive researcher she has continued to work on the letters and gave a fascinating talk on them at Linslade in May 2009 which we attended. We are grateful to her for providing us with information about the children of the marriage.

Chapter 7

38. Flaxman Ted & Joan, "Cottisford MIs", 2006, pp. 5, 6 & 31

39. Hearne Archive. R Frisby's account dated 4th January 1799 for £22-14s-6d to Revd Mr Cotton for wines and spirits, Photo 0736

40. Ibid. John Day's inventory dated 8th April 1799 of the late Dr Cotton's effects at Tingewick, Photos 0753 to 0771

41. Ibid. Wm Gunn's account dated 31 January 1801 for £5-15s-0d to Rev Charles Cotton for odd jobs covering the period January 1795 to March 1799, Photos 0702 and 0711

42. Ibid. Thos Harvey's account of 31st March 1799 for £7-7s-0d to Rev Mr Cotton for two coffins, Photo 0718

43. Ibid. Philip and Thomas Box's account of 29th October 1798 for £13-18s-9d to the

Executors of the late The Revd Mr Cotton for undertakers' expenses, Photo 0703

44. Ibid. Philip and Thomas Box's two accounts of 21st March 1799 for £18-15s-4d and £10-16s-8d to the Executors of the late The Revd Mr Cotton for undertakers' expenses, Photos 0717 and 0720

Chapter 8

45. "A history of Oxfordshire – Ploughley Hundred", Victoria County History, Volume VI, Oxford University Press, 1959, p. 106

46. "Despatches from England", Vols XX to XXIII, 1710 to 1721, Madras Record Office, Superintendent Govt Press, 1927, 14th March 1715, p.60

47n. We have generally adopted the spelling "Cossimbazar" for this place, but there are many variants. The standard work on British India, known as Hobson Jobson (which is available on line), uses that spelling but says that it was properly Kasimbazar – "a town no longer existing, which closely adjoined the city of Murshidabad, but preceded the latter". Also known as Castle Bazaar and Kassembasar.

48. "Collections of Travels, &c; being the Travels of Monsieur Tavernier, Bernier, and other great men" in 2 vols, folio, London, 1684 [ed. by V A Ball, 2 vols, London, 1889]

49. IOR G/23/5, "Kasimbazar Consultations 1733–1740", 21st November 1738

50. IOR P/174/90, "Journal Bengal 1713–1714", p. 178

51. IOR G/23/5, "Kasimbazar Consultations 1733–1740", Charges general for December 1738 and December 1739

52. IOR G/23/5, "Kasimbazar Consultations 1733–1740", 14th January 1738/9

53. IOR G/23/5, "Kasimbazar Consultations 1733–1740", 14th January 1738/9, Officers and Soldiers pay

54. IOR P/174/90, "Journal Bengal 1713–1714", p. 10

55. IOR G/23/5, "Kasimbazar Consultations 1733–1740", 28th March 1740

56. IOR G/23/5, "Kasimbazar Consultations 1733–1740", 1st January 1739/40

57. Records of Fort St George, "Diary and Consultation Book for 1721", pp. 170-201

58. IOR G/23/5, "Kasimbazar Consultations 1733–1740", 21st November 1738

59. IOR P/1/7, "Bengal Public Consultations 1729–30, 24th January 1729/30

60. IOR G/23/5, "Kasimbazar Consultations 1733–1740", 13th December 1738

61. IOR G/23/5, "Kasimbazar Consultations 1733–1740", 3rd June 1739

62. IOR G/23/5, "Kasimbazar Consultations 1733–1740", 14th January 1738/39

63. IOR G/23/5, "Kasimbazar Consultations 1733–1740", 27th April 1739

64. IOR P/174/90, "Journal Bengal 1713–1714", p. 176

65. Personal communication, Margaret Makepeace, Senior Archivist, British Library, 23rd February 2006

66. IOR G/23/6, "Kasimbazar Consultations 1741–1744", 4th December 1740

67. IOR G/23/6, "Kasimbazar Consultations 1741–1744", 20th December 1740

68. IOR G/23/6, "Kasimbazar Consultations 1741–1744", 20th January 1740/41

69. IOR G/23/6, "Kasimbazar Consultations 1741–1744", 7th February 1740/41

70. IOR G/23/6, "Kasimbazar Consultations 1741–1744", 24th March 1740/41

71. "Bengal Past and Present", Vol XXVII, Part 1, Calcutta Historical Society , P C Ray, 1924, p. 41

72. IOR G/23/6, "Kasimbazar Consultations 1741–1744", 15th February 1742/43

73. IOR G/23/6, "Kasimbazar Consultations 1741–1744", 15th March 1742/43

74. "Bengal Past and Present", Vol XXVII, Part 1, Calcutta Historical Society , P C Ray, 1924, p. 41

75. Burnell J, "Bombay in the days of Queen Anne, to which is added Burnell's narrative of his adventures in Bengal", London, Hakluyt Society, 1933

76. IOR P/174/90, "Journal Bengal 1713–1714", p. 184

77n. Although there is no evidence associating Richard Eyre with the practice, slavery evidently occurred in British India at that time. The Will of Dorothy King, widow of a British mariner, made in December 1711 included the following: "Item to my slave Sarah I give full Freedom and liberty and to my Brother in Law Mr Francis Wadden's Widow I bequeath my Slave Boy Tom desiring my Slave Dye may be sold as part of my Estate". Bengal Public Consultation P/1/2, 1701–1715. p. 50 (also 286)

78. Phillimore's parish registers series, Volume 121, Middlesex Vol 1, Hanwell, p. 103

79. Eland G (Editor), "Purefoy Letters 1735–53", Volume 2, London, Sidgwick & Jackson Ltd, 1931, p. 285

80. Hill S C, "List of Europeans in Siege of Calcutta 1756", Calcutta, 1902, OIR 920.054, p. 37

81n. It seems likely that this Mr Justice Blackstone, mentioned in the Will of Martha Eyre, was Sir William Blackstone, author of the celebrated "Commentaries on the Laws of England" and first Vinerian Professor of Law at Oxford. His wife Sarah had, like Martha Eyre, formerly been a Clitherow

Chapter 9

82. Eton College archive, Map No 51.116

83n. Flora Thompson referred to the married schoolteacher as Mrs Tenby, "Lark Rise", p. 186

Chapter 11

84n. In the second generation, Edwards Rousby moved out of Cottisford House for a short period in the early 1850s and was living with his wife at Irthlingborough when their first child was born in 1855. See also References 92 and 93.

85n. In Jackson's Oxford Journal of 6th March 1830 the sale by auction was advertised at Souldern House later that month of household furniture and livestock the property of J E Rousby Esq. We have found no evidence of whether or not that sale took place, but there is clearly a possibility that the family did not move direct from Souldern to Cottisford.

86n. In "The Era, London Gazettes" for 5th June 1842 a Henry Rousby of Park Terrace, Park Road, Regents Park appeared in a list of Insolvent Debtors Petitions. Whether or not this was Henry, the son of James Edwards Rousby, has not been discovered.

87n. "The St Bees College Calendar for the year 1858" London, F&J Rivington, 1858. This shows that the course lasted a minimum of two years, "this period being divided into four Terms; during which, residence is indispensable". Fees for tuition were £10 a Term and each student was required to furnish himself with a house or lodgings in the village. "The expense of board and lodgings, with moderate economy, may be from eighteen shillings to twenty four shillings a week for each Student". Before any application for admission to the College could be entertained each student had to furnish a Testimonial from a Clergyman of the Church of England certifying "after a long and intimate acquaintance" that the applicant was "a man of unblemished morality and consistent piety" specifying "as well his pursuits from the time when he left school to that in which the certificate is granted".

88n. Arthur Rousby died intestate. The Grant of Probate to his widow Elizabeth on 6th July 1864 assessed him as being worth "under £20" at the time of his death and she eventually took on the role of lodging-house keeper. His elder son, also named Arthur, was none the less able to describe himself as a "Gentleman" at the time of the 1881 Census when he was aged 23. Both the younger children, then aged 20 and 18, gave their occupations as "Nothing". Twenty years later, in 1901, the elder son was still able to describe himself as "Living on own means".

89n. Although Gregory was a country parson – at Tansor in Northamptonshire – at the time of his marriage to Emily Rousby in 1850 he had previously experienced a very different life. In September 1839 he had sailed from London with his first wife, Emma, bound for Tasmania. The voyage took five months and he became Crown Chaplain in what was known at that time as Van Diemens Land, living at Oatlands, midway between Hobart and Launceston. Today this small community of about 500 inhabitants boasts one of the finest collections of surviving Georgian stone houses in Australia. At the time when Gregory Bateman was there the population of Tasmania was c. 45,000, of whom at least 10,000 were convicts transported there from England. It is recorded that when the roof of one of the houses in Oatlands was being constructed the work was carried out by two convicts, both wearing leg irons. Gregory Bateman's first wife died in Australia and he returned to England in 1847.

90. "St Denys Church, Cold Ashby – A Brief History", leaflet available in the church

91n. "Gentleman" on their Marriage Certificate 1858, "Bank Manager" on Lucy's Death Certificate 1906

92. Blomfield Rev J C, "History of Cottisford, Hardwick and Tusmore", J W Arrowsmith, Bristol, 1857, p. 24

93. Oxfordshire Record Office, Brown and Merry papers, ACC905

94. Private communication from Lesley Whitelaw, Archivist, Middle Temple library, 11th December 2007

95n. The father of Rudolph, Henry de Salis, had been born in Italy and was described as a Count of the Holy Roman Empire. Rudolph was educated at Eton from 1868 to 1871 and Trinity Hall, Cambridge from 1874 to 1876. He was then apprenticed to a Civil Engineer from 1877 to 1880 and obtained Associate Membership of the Institution of Civil Engineers in April 1880. His only recorded contribution to the Proceedings of the Institution was in 1884/85 when he spoke at considerable length in a discussion on the possibility of changing from the Imperial System of measurement to the Metric System. He was strongly against such a change, his reasons being many and varied. He conceded that the Metric or Decimal System was much easier to learn, but thought "surely that was not altogether an advantage … in point of mental training". He resigned his membership of the Institution at the end of 1890 when he was 35 years of age (information from the Institution's archivist).

96. Kelly's Directory of Buckinghamshire, 1895, p. 161

97. Thompson F J, "Lark Rise", Chapter XII, pp. 194–5, 197

98n. E R K Rousby may well have "taken his responsibilities less seriously than his mother did hers" but he did purchase the freehold of Cottisford House in 1884–85 from Eton College. In a letter dated 7th April 1885 on completion of the sale his solicitor asked the College's solicitors a question which seems distinctly odd today - "must we bring cash or will you accept our cheque for "£5,655-13s-9d purchase money and interest"? Eton College archives, Bundle No 133a, 1884, Oxford

99. Thompson F J, "Lark Rise", Chapter XII, p. 198

100n. We are indebted to Charles Jackson of Cottisford House for drawing to our attention the 1896 mortgage document and allowing us to photograph it.

101n. The Victoria County History of Oxfordshire (Vol VI page 107) states that E R K Rousby "was succeeded by his son F R Rousby". That must surely be incorrect. Birth Registrations record no child of his brief marriage and neither E R K Rousby nor Agnes Lilian, in their Wills of 1927 and 1942 respectively, made any mention of offspring. He left most of his estate to his surviving sister, Josephine Worley: Agnes Lilian left the whole of her estate to her sister.

Chapter 12

102n. Gaskell E, "Oxfordshire leaders: social and political", London: the Queenhithe Printing and Publishing Co, no date. In a personal communication of 12th December 2007 The Centre for Oxfordshire studies estimate the date as around 1907

103. "Yorkshire East Riding", Victoria County History, Volume VIII, 2008, p. 185

104n. The relationship of R J Clay is incorrectly stated on the memorial – he was actually a *great* nephew. A 21-year-old sister, Ann Rousby, of Henry and Robert had married James Naish at Hawton in 1705. Her daughter Elizabeth Naish of Bilsthorpe married John Clay gent by licence in 1727 and Robert James Clay was their son, baptised at St Mary Magdalene church, Newark in 1732.

105. University of Hull Archives, Document Ref DDSY/9/22, Affidavit of John Swails senior of Croom farmer

106. University of Hull Archives, Document Ref DDSY/9/25, Affidavit of Richard Batchelor of Westbury, gent

107n. Martha Peckover Edwards Rousby, one of the sisters of Henry Edwards Rousby, was married at Great Driffield to John Kendall on 17th July 1808 when she was 21. Information from "An index of Marriage Bonds and Allegations in the Peculiar Jurisdiction of the Dean and Chapter of York,1613–1839" p. 146

108. "Yorkshire East Riding", Victoria County History, Volume VIII, 2008, p. 22

109. Fairfax J, "Sykes of Sledmere: the record of a sporting family and famous stud", Blakeborough, 1929, p. 22

110. Country Life, 16th January, 1986

111. University of Hull Archives, Document Ref DDSY/9/24, Papers in Chancery Suit, John Kendall and others v. Samuel Vines and others, p. 21

112. Ibid, pp. 41 & 42

Chapter 13

113. Thompson F J, "Lark Rise", Chapter V, p. 79

114. Blomfield Rev J C, "History of Lower and Upper Heyford", Elliot Stock, London, 1892

115. "Plan of the Open and Common Fields and the Inclosures of Cottisford in the County of Oxford", Eton College Archives, 51/116

116. "A history of Oxfordshire – Ploughley Hundred", Victoria County History, Volume VI, Oxford University Press, 1959, p. 112

117. "An Act to authorise the Inclosure of certain Lands in pursuance of a Special Report of the Inclosure Commissioners for England and Wales", AD 1848, 11&12 Victoriae, CAP CIX

118. Eton College Archives, COLL/EST/COTT/7 Item 4B5/4

119. Eton College Archives, COLL/EST/COTT/7 Item 4C5/5

120. Eton College Archives, COLL/EST/COTT/7 Item 4C5/10

121n. The account of successive stages in the Enclosure which follows comes largely from reports in Jackson's Oxford Journal

122. Oxfordshire Record Office, Cottisford Enclosure Award, Book 23

123n. Rev David Erskine Dewar, though Curate of Cottisford for only a short period (1851–52) was probably appointed to cover the death or incapacity of the Rector, Francis Hodgson, prior to the arrival of Rev Charles Harrison as Rector. He was already Rector of Edgcott 10 miles (16 km) away to the east. He was the second son of Sir James Dewar, Chief Justice of Bombay, and he married here in July 1852 Elizabeth Anne Fane Parry, the daughter of J B Parry Esq QC (who occupied Cottisford House for a few years – see References 84n, 92 and 93 above).

124. Thompson F J, "Lark Rise", Chapter 1, p. 27

Chapter 14

125. "A history of Oxfordshire – Ploughley Hundred", Victoria County History, Volume VI, Oxford University Press, 1959, pp. 337–338

126. Thompson F J, "Lark Rise", Chapter X, pp.155–165 and Chapter XV p. 247

127n. William Cripps died on 7th March 1909 and the death certificate, based on information provided by his son William, shows him as still having lived at 24 Low Lackenby and his occupation as "Labourer at Blast furnaces".

128. Personal communication, 3rd January 2009, from Stuart Pacitto, Archives Northeast

129. Thompson F J, "Lark Rise", Chapter I, p. 21 and Chapter III p. 62

130. Lindsay G, "Flora Thompson – The story of the Lark Rise writer", second edition, John Owen Smith, Headley Down, 2007, pp. 79 & 80

131. Thompson F J, "Lark Rise", Chapter X, p. 166

132. Lindsay G, "Flora Thompson – The story of the Lark Rise writer", second edition, John Owen Smith, Headley Down, 2007, p. 80

133. Thompson F J, "Lark Rise", Chapter V, pp. 96–97

Chapter 15

134n. Rev Statham, writing as "S.M.S". in a local newspaper under the headline "THE WAR"! contributed an obituary of Edwin Timms in about August 1916 . In this he mentioned that Edwin Timms had attended service in Cottisford church while home on leave only eight weeks before, and also the severe wounding of William Cross. Press cutting at the Old Gaol Museum, Buckingham, copy kindly provided by Tony Webster

135n. 305 men of the Battalion went into Turkish captivity but only 92 survived. Sydney Gaskin died at Adana in southern Turkey but was buried in Baghdad. See "Banbury Guardian", 25th December 1919

136. Flaxman Ted & Joan, "Cottisford Revisited", second edition, 2008, p. 54

Chapter 16

137n. Much of the detailed personal information in this chapter, and several of the photographs, have been kindly provided by Captain Philip Brooke-Popham, only son of Sir Robert. See also "Acknowledgements".

138. Personal communication from Stuart Hadaway, Assistant Curator, RAF Museum Hendon, 3rd October 2008

139. Chronicle 1953, Volume LV, The Ox and Bucks Light Infantry Chronicle. pp. 242–247

140. Brooke-Popham papers in the Rhodes Library, Item III/3/38

141. Personal communication from Stuart Hadaway, Assistant Curator, RAF Museum Hendon, 1st June 2009

142. Brooke-Popham papers in the Rhodes Library, Item III/3/24, letter dated 6th December 1937, p. 2

143. Brooke-Popham papers in the Rhodes Library, Item III/10/11, 15th March 1944

144. Flaxman Ted & Joan, "Cottisford MIs", 2006, pp. 15 & 27

145. Oxford Times (East), 30th October 1953, p. 7

Chapter 17

146. Woodman R, "The Real Cruel Sea: The Merchant Navy in the Battle of the Atlantic 1939–43", John Murray, 2005, pp. 360 & 367

147. Edwards B, "Attack and Sink!: the battle for convoy SC42", Wimborne Minster, Dorset, New Guild, 1995

148. Personal communication 12th October 2007 from Richard Woodman providing details of *MV Jedmoor*

149. Commonwealth War Graves Commission information, also listed in the chapel at the National Memorial Arboretum

150. Card Index of Lloyds List from 1927, Guildhall Library, four cards 1938–1941, *"Jedmoor"* No 160507

151n. Much of the information about the last voyage of the *Jedmoor* in this chapter comes from reference 147 above, which describes in detail the week-long battle for this one convoy.

152. "The story of St Petrox Church Dartmouth" – leaflet available in the church.

Chapter 18

153. Thompson F J, "Lark Rise to Candleford", Film and TV tie-in edition, published by Penguin, 2008

154. Dewhurst K, "Lark Rise to Candleford", Hutchinson, 1980, pp. 19–93

155. Ibid, pp. 94–171

156n. Hideko Ishida, whose Japanese version of "Lark Rise" was published in 2008, ISBN 978-4-86085-068-5

157. Thompson F J, "Lark Rise to Candleford", Chapter V, p. 88

158. Ibid, Chapter XIV, p. 212

159. Ibid, Chapter XV, p. 247

Chapter 19

160. Lindsay G, "Flora Thompson – The story of the Lark Rise writer", second edition, John Owen Smith, Headley Down, 2007, p. 99

161n. When ships of the Royal Navy were lost during the Second World War the facts were almost invariably made public immediately. But details of the loss of merchant vessels were deliberately not published once they started to mount alarmingly in mid-1940. The scale of the menace created and the sinking of more than 2,800 merchant ships – largely in the years 1940–43 and mainly by U-boats – were not revealed until afterwards when the danger had passed. The general public did not know at the time that 35,000 merchant seamen had died in the crucial task of keeping this country supplied during the war. They were all civilians, all volunteers like Peter Thompson, merely trying to do their accustomed job – some killed by sudden explosions, some drowned, some burnt alive in blazing tankers and some dying from thirst, hunger and exposure after days, weeks or even months on rafts or in open boats. See Terraine J, "Business in Great Waters", Wordsworth, 1999, p. 669

162. Lindsay G, "Flora Thompson – The story of the Lark Rise writer", John Owen Smith, Headley Down, 2007, pp. 174–175

163n. Flora Thompson refers several times to residents of Juniper Hill making a point of "not flinching", for instance in "Lark Rise" on page 50 and most notably on page 247

ACKNOWLEDGEMENTS

During the preparation of this, our third booklet, we have had the pleasure of meeting and/or corresponding with many people who have an interest in the history of this Parish. They have been helpful in many different ways, some recounting their memories and others providing us with documents, photographs, etc, all of which help to fill in the human details of times past. We should like to record our gratitude to all of the following:

Collette Allen, Sue Baxter, Donald Barker, Father A J Burns, the late Laurence Butler, Gwynneth Clark, Jackie Cleaves, Ron Collins, the late Joan Cottrell, Tony Cripps, Michael Cross, Keith Dewhurst, Barbara English, John Flaxman, Liz and Maurice Gilbert, Maureen Greatbatch, Sylvia Hasam, Charles Jackson, Gillian Lindsay, Irene Lomas, Rita Lomas, Jean Morris, Julian Munby, David Neave, Miriam Parsley, Margaret Selfridge, Heather Thorn, Kathy Upex, Antonio Venditto, Ron Vickers, Mary Watkins, Dulcie and Michael Watts, Tony Webster and Richard Woodman

In addition, we must record our particular gratitude to two individuals who have supplied us with detailed information on major topics which we could not otherwise have covered adequately.

First, in August 2006 Diana and Philip Brooke-Popham paid a visit here and signed the visitors book in the church. This prompted us to contact them, leading to fruitful correspondence and then, eventually, a visit to Bagborough House where we met Philip, the only son of Sir Robert Brooke-Popham, himself now a Captain RN, retired. He was able to provide us with a great deal of personal information about the family's time at Cottisford House and also allowed us the use of several family photographs in Chapter 16. For all his help we are most grateful.

Secondly, after we had given a talk about Cottisford to Tingewick Historical Society in March 2007 we were told by their Chairman, Anthony Houghton-Brown, of a remarkable collection of documents, some of them more than 200 years old, which had survived from a solicitor's office in Buckingham. These contain material of considerable interest relating to this Parish and he kindly made arrangements for us to see them and take digital photographs. Much of the material in Chapters 5 and 7, plus Appendix C, comes from these papers and we are indebted to Anthony for allowing us access to this unique and unexpected treasure trove.

Our researches have extended to the following record offices and libraries where we have received a great deal of help from staff: Berkshire Record Office, Borthwick Institute for Archives, Bristol Record Office, Buckinghamshire Record Office, Centre for Oxfordshire Studies, Centre for Banburyshire Studies, Cheshire Record Office, Commonwealth War Graves Commission, East Riding Record Office, Eton College Archives, Gwent Record Office, Imperial War Museum, Institution of Civil Engineers, Lancashire Record Office, Leicestershire Record Office, London Metropolitan Archives, Middle Temple, Northamptonshire Record Office, Nottinghamshire Record Office, Oxfordshire Record Office, Probate Office, RAF Museum, Society of Genealogists, St Bees Theological College, Surrey Record Centre, Swindon and Wiltshire History Centre, Teesside Record Office, Trinity College Oxford Archives, University of Glasgow Archives, University of Hull Archives; Bicester library, The Bodleian library, Brackley library, the British library, Buckingham library, Canterbury library, the Guildhall library, Northampton library, Oxford reference library, Lambeth Palace library, Rhodes library, Southport library, State of Tasmania library and York library.

We must particularly thank Penny Hatfield, the Archivist at Eton College, and her staff. The College's ownership of this Parish for more than four centuries resulted in a large quantity of documents, such as leases and associated correspondence, being generated. The resulting archive has been invaluable to researchers over the years, notably to Rev Blomfield in the 19th Century and to the authors of the Victoria County History in the 20th Century. Effective indexing greatly enhances the usefulness of this archive and we are glad to be able to include in this volume copies of three unusual documents which are probably not widely known – the late 18th-Century map of the Parish showing clearly the last remnants of the original medieval strips (figs. 37 & 38, pp. 50–53); the colourful plan of Cuckolds Burrows (ECR 26/289 – fig 88, p. 48); and the important letter from Rev Dewar in 1851 about the proposed enclosure of the Heath (fig 53, p. 56). All of these are reproduced by permission of the Provost and Fellows of Eton College.

We must also thank the following for permission to reproduce documents: The Bodleian Library for figure 60; The British Library for figures 31 and 32; Gwent Record Office and the incumbent of Kemys for figure 14; Oxfordshire Record Office for figures 42 and 55 and also Rev Christobel Hargreaves, Rector of the Shelswell Benefice, for figure 42; and Penguin Books for Figure 81. And we must acknowledge Buckingham Record Office as the source of figures 17–20, 22 and 23; Hull University Archives as the source of figure 52; and the Centre for Oxfordshire Studies as the source of figures 10–13, 27, 35, 39, 40, 47, 54 and 56.

Oxfordshire is a particularly good county in which to carry out historical research. It has two excellent facilities in the Centre for Oxfordshire Studies in the Westgate Centre (for published material) and the Oxfordshire Record Office at Cowley (for primary material). Both are blessed with helpful staff. In addition, Oxford houses the huge resource of the Bodleian Library at several different sites in the city. Not every county is so fortunate.

Cherwell District Council have again made a contribution towards production costs. We appreciate their continuing support for local initiatives of this kind.

We are grateful to Michael Prior for improving three of the pictures and to Clare Carr for producing the graphs in Chapter 14. When the draft of this booklet was approaching finality it was read through by Margaret Allen and Judith Allen, both of whom picked up errors and inconsistencies. We are grateful to them for this, but responsibility for any remaining mistakes is, of course, ours.

Finally we must express our warm thanks to Sir Hugo Brunner, not only for writing the Foreword but also for making several helpful comments and suggestions. His enthusiasm for Flora Thompson's writings and his capacious knowledge of Oxfordshire make his support especially valuable and we much appreciate it.